What people are saying about …

UNCENSORED

"Those who are committed to living, believing, and embracing 'the whole counsel of God' are never at liberty to sift through verses, discarding those less desirable to our thinking and personal philosophy. Brian Cosby does an excellent job of demonstrating the danger and unhealthy consequences to our Christian faith if we choose to ignore or censor difficult portions of Scripture. *Uncensored* is a clear call to embrace the whole of Scripture so that it will capture your heart and mind, radically driving you forward in your Christian journey."

Steven J. Lawson, president of
OnePassion Ministries and professor of
preaching at The Master's Seminary

"In my own Christian life, I know how it can be all too easy to ignore difficult passages in favor of ones that are encouraging. This is why Dr. Brian Cosby wrote his excellent new book, *Uncensored*. This book will help readers learn how to live their lives under the authority of the Word of God. I highly recommend this book and believe as you read the contents it will help you grow in your knowledge of, love for, and enjoyment of living by God's Word."

Dave Jenkins, executive director
of Servants of Grace Ministries and
executive editor of *Theology for Life*

"We believe that the Bible is God's Word—not just the parts we like and can explain easily—the whole thing. But sometimes we're stumped by questions we're asked, or ask ourselves, when we read the Bible. *Uncensored* is a sensible, accessible, and informed guide to help us have greater confidence in God's Word. This book will give you a new appreciation for how all the pieces of the Bible fit together into a coherent story."

Michael Horton, professor of theology at Westminster Seminary California and author of *The Christian Faith: A Systematic Theology for Pilgrims on the Way*

"If we are honest, most of us would admit that we have—at some time or another—stumbled across those portions of Scripture that have left us confused (even troubled) regarding their precise meaning and place in the Bible. Additionally, most of us have had uncomfortable conversations with family members, friends, and coworkers who have insisted that they do not believe in the God of the Bible on account of particular verses or subjects in Scripture. In the postmodern and pluralistic society in which we live, there is a dire need for us to understand the more challenging passages and subjects of Scripture and to be able to intelligently explain them to others. Whether it is the doctrine of creation or the doctrine of hell, the problem of evil, the redemptive-historical structure of Scripture regarding the Law of God, or the Bible's teaching about the role of husbands and wives, Brian Cosby has given us a guide to help us read the Bible *uncensored.*"

Nicholas T. Batzig, organizing pastor of New Covenant Presbyterian Church, Richmond Hill, Georgia, and editor of *The Christward Collective*

UNCENSORED

UNCENSORED

Daring to Embrace the Entire Bible

BRIAN COSBY

David C Cook®
transforming lives together

UNCENSORED
Published by David C Cook
4050 Lee Vance View
Colorado Springs, CO 80918 U.S.A.

David C Cook Distribution Canada
55 Woodslee Avenue, Paris, Ontario, Canada N3L 3E5

David C Cook U.K., Kingsway Communications
Eastbourne, East Sussex BN23 6NT, England

The graphic circle C logo is a registered trademark of David C Cook.

The website addresses recommended throughout this book are offered as a
resource to you. These websites are not intended in any way to be or imply an
endorsement on the part of David C Cook, nor do we vouch for their content.

Unless otherwise noted, all Scripture quotations are taken from The Holy
Bible, English Standard Version® (ESV®), copyright © 2001 by Crossway, a
publishing ministry of Good News Publishers. Used by permission. All rights
reserved. Scripture quotations marked NIV are taken from the Holy Bible, New
International Version®, NIV®. Copyright © 1973, 2011 by Biblica, Inc.® Used by
permission of Zondervan. All rights reserved worldwide. www.zondervan.com.
The author has added italics to Scripture quotations for emphasis.

LCCN 2015940469
ISBN 978-1-4347-0909-7
eISBN 978-0-7814-1369-5

The Team: Tim Peterson, Keith Wall, Amy Konyndyk, Jack Campbell, Karen Athen
Cover Design: Nick Lee
Cover Photo: Shutterstock

Printed in the United States of America
First Edition 2015

1 2 3 4 5 6 7 8 9 10

072815

To

The elders of Wayside Presbyterian Church (PCA)
for your unashamed commitment to
embracing the entire Bible

CONTENTS

FOREWORD

The Bible is the divinely inspired and totally truthful Word of God. Psalm 119, the longest chapter in the Bible, is a paean to God's revealed Word: "I seek you with all my heart; do not let me stray from your commands," the psalmist declared. "I have hidden your word in my heart that I might not sin against you. Praise be to you, LORD; teach me your decrees.... Your statutes are my delight; they are my counselors" (Ps. 119:10–12, 24 NIV). God's Word gave birth to the church, and God continues to sustain and nourish His people through His Word and by His Spirit. But the Bible has never been without controversy within the church itself. Three great "battles for the Bible" have marked the history of the Christian church.

The struggle for the *integrity* of the Bible arose in the second century AD through the work of a heretic named Marcion. Marcion was struck by the radical newness of Jesus, a point made by the apostle Paul in 2 Corinthians 5:17. But he divorced this valid biblical insight from the total compass of biblical revelation. Because Jesus has made everything new, Marcion said, we don't need the *Old* Testament anymore. Let's rip it out of our Bibles! In response to Marcion, the church emphasized the integrity of Scripture and, over time, was led by the Holy Spirit to recognize the prophetic and apostolic writings that constitute the canon of Scripture.

At the time of the Reformation, the question of the Bible's *authority* became a church-dividing issue between Catholics and Protestants. Martin Luther, John Calvin, and other Reformers emphasized the normative authority of Scripture over church councils, papal pronouncements, and other traditions in the history of the church. The Bible is the definitive norm by which everything else must be normed. *Suprema Scriptura!*

The age of the Enlightenment brought another great watershed in biblical understanding, as radical skeptics called into question the *veracity* of the events and miracles recorded in the Bible. In this context it became necessary to assert anew that the Bible was totally truthful, without error in all that it affirmed. This means, quite simply, that in the Bible the history is historical and the miracles are miraculous.

Brian Cosby is a Presbyterian pastor who teaches and preaches the Bible week by week. He is well acquainted with the historic debates about the Bible I have referred to in the preceding paragraphs. He knows their continuing importance for the life of the church today. But in this book he is primarily concerned with another, more recent issue, namely the propensity of many contemporary Christians—including many pastors—to cherry-pick favorite passages and themes in the Bible to the exclusion (or at least the downplaying) of others. This phenomenon cuts across traditional liberal-conservative divisions in the church and applies to everyone who reads, studies, and preaches from the Scriptures. The Bible, Cosby suggests, is being *censored*—not so much by ecclesiastical inquisitors or by unbelieving scholars (though many examples of such can be cited), but by our own cultural accommodations, prejudices, and spiritual blindness. We need to heed Cosby's warning at this point.

There is a place for apologetics, and it is good to be always ready "to give an answer" to anyone who wants to know why we as followers of Jesus Christ believe what we do (1 Pet. 3:15 NIV). But even more than that, what is needed today is a faithfulness to declare the whole counsel of God, to read and believe the entire Bible as the metanarrative of God's dealings with the world and with His people in judgment and love, along with an unfeigned courage to declare the gospel—God's good news—to everyone everywhere. Only in this way will the people of God "be thoroughly equipped for every good work" and come to know and love the Bible as "useful for teaching, rebuking, correcting, and training in righteousness" (2 Tim. 3:16–17 NIV).

Timothy George
founding dean of Beeson Divinity
School of Samford University,
general editor of the Reformation
Commentary on Scripture series

PART ONE

EMBARRASSED BY THE BIBLE

1

THE MCFARMER BURGER

I swallowed a big blue sleeping pill to knock me out. I had envisioned riding on a train to be something akin to taking a trip on the Polar Express. But I found the bumps and sways rather unnerving.

As the train plunged beneath the English Channel in a tube connecting England to France, I settled back in my seat, wondering if the civil engineers had triple-checked the seams along the walls. All I could think was, *Just don't dwell on it.* But alas, the big blue pill plunged me further into a twilight zone, and the bumps became a gentle massage under me.

In the hours that followed—groggy and reeling from my baptismal Chunnel experience—I downed a Red Bull and a Twix and began searching for something to do. Unfortunately, trains don't have *SkyMall* magazines, so I pulled out my Fodor's travel guide.

I was heading to Interlaken, Switzerland, to do some backpacking and to take a much-needed break from my studies in London.

A once-in-a-lifetime trip, for sure, but I was also plunging into serious debt.

As I licked the last remnants of chocolate from my fingers, I began reading about all the quaint Swiss cantons, the rolling hills, and the majestic Alps separating northern and southern Europe. I envisioned the beautiful sunsets around Interlaken and the snowy charm of medieval castles.

After arriving, I hustled through the blustery snow straight to my hostel. Hostels (as Forrest Gump might say) are like a box of chocolates: you never know what you're going to get. Upon entering my room, I surveyed my roommates. Some had long beards and were eager to tell even longer stories. A strange odor drifted from two travel-weary women who had left their shoes back somewhere in Middle-earth.

After a few niceties and smiles, I put my pack in a prepaid locker and went exploring. I spotted a pub not far away, but just before entering, two men staggered outside throwing punches. I froze. Ready to intervene—unsure how exactly—I realized that the short, elderly fellow was fending off his younger assailant just fine. *This isn't in my travel guide*, I thought.

As it turned out, Interlaken uncovered a whole side of her that never graced the pages of my Fodor's guidebook. Some parts of the city were dirty and other parts seemed embarrassing (like the man relieving himself off the train platform). Did you know that the McDonald's offers a McFarmer Burger? It's true. And when I told some locals that I came from Tennessee, they smiled at me as if I were their best friend and called out, "*Ja!* Jack Daniel's!"

AM I EMBARRASSED BY THE BIBLE?

When it comes to the Bible, American evangelicalism is often like my travel guide. It presents a glowing presentation of the biblical text—highlighting well-loved favorites across radio waves and billboards—while leaving out those scriptural passages that might be offensive or embarrassing.

To be sure, the Bible contains many hard-to-swallow texts. Israelites stoned adulterers. Slaves were told to obey their masters. Jesus taught that sinners go to hell. At God's command, His people killed both young and old, even animals. The Bible is brimming with passages that make many Christians blush, squirm, and cringe.

I've been there too.

Recently, as I flipped through the Psalms in my Bible, I noticed something disturbing. I had underlined and highlighted those passages that communicated God's steadfast love, His gracious care, and the joyful praise of His people. At times, my red pen seemed to hum along in a triumphal ink-letting *until* I hit "Oh that you would slay the wicked, O God" (Ps. 139:19).

That's when it stopped. My pen did a hop, skip, and jump to "and lead me in the way everlasting" (v. 24). Looking through other portions of my Bible, I noticed the same trend. From Genesis to Malachi, Matthew to Revelation, it seemed as though I didn't want to read the offensive and edgy. I didn't want to ponder the scientific improbability of the sun standing still (Josh. 10:13) or why the man with crushed testicles wasn't allowed to enter the assembly of worship (Deut. 23:1).

Am I embarrassed by the Bible?

If the Bible is truly inspired by God—as His self-revelation—and profitable for His people, then I should embrace the *whole* counsel of God for a healthy, balanced, and fruit-filled faith. When I censor the Scriptures and selectively choose which parts to meditate on, day and night, I fail to become that tree planted by streams of water, bearing fruit in its season (Ps. 1:1–3). I miss out on the life-altering and joy-infusing revelation of God, which is living and active (Heb. 4:12).

THE GRAVY

As a retired Vietnam vet, Russell spends his time fishing, working on his '98 Silverado, and setting the clocks twice a year at the church. In the evenings—if there is nothing better on—he and his wife watch TV preachers until they ask for "seed" money, at which point he interjects, "Those preachers are thieves!" I agree.

Russell takes pride in two things: being a backwoods, "red state," gun-toting southerner and the fact that he's a self-proclaimed "John 3:16 man." He once told me over some hotcakes at IHOP, "John 3:16 is all that matters. The other stuff is just gravy." He's often hinted that while he may not *know* all the Ten Commandments, at least he *keeps* them. While I certainly love John 3:16 and the Ten Commandments, I've grown increasingly concerned about how we handle the "other stuff"—the gravy.

In a nearby town, a man named Charles—who might be Russell's long-lost cousin—started attending a new men's Bible study I helped lead. After several weeks, Charles became uneasy about our topics, as I was teaching through "difficult" themes of the Bible. On one

November morning, I introduced the imprecatory psalms—those prayers and petitions invoking judgment upon God's enemies.

"I'm through!" Charles hollered.

Later, he asked if we could meet, and we talked through the sobering topic of God's justice. As uneasy as that conversation was, the experience shed light on a bigger problem within the church and in my own life: many self-professing Christians cherry-pick the Scriptures for a feel-good faith.

I have unintentionally ignored various passages in the Bible, and I have also come to realize that I've unintentionally inserted my own "revelation" into the biblical text. Or is it unintentional?

If you listen closely to our Christianese, you will notice a large amount of *extra*biblical thought squeezed in. Try to find "God helps those who help themselves," "Invite Jesus into your heart," or "Accept Jesus as your personal Lord and Savior" in the Bible. They're not there. Not only are we cherry-picking the Scriptures, but we're also inserting our own feel-good notions.

In an effort to be successful, to be the big church on the block, or to gain a respected foothold in the eyes of the watching world, we have compromised our affirmation, belief, and proclamation that *all* Scripture—not some—is God breathed, holy, and profitable for His people (2 Tim. 3:16). We like the *idea* of being biblical—"We're a biblical church!"—but have functionally censored portions of Scripture.

The question remains: Can the church continue to cling to a fig-leaf faith—uncomfortable by the edgy and seemingly archaic—or is it time to unashamedly embrace the God-inspired, Christ-exalting, and life-transforming truth of the entire Bible, offensive passages and all?

AN EXCITING JOURNEY

You are about to set out on a journey that promises to foster deep joy and God-honoring trust. An incomplete Word leads to incomplete joy. Why would we settle for an incomplete text when every jot and tittle is inspired by our great God? This is a journey to embrace the Bible—the *entire* Bible—every book, every verse, and every word. It's both daring and exciting.

Maybe you've chased a feel-good faith by extracting those warm and fuzzy and socially acceptable Bible verses we find plastered on bumper stickers and social media. And maybe, like me, you don't even realize you're doing it. That's what this book is about. In the pages that follow, we'll explore the landscape of the cherry-picking church and what we can do to joyfully and trustingly embrace the entire Bible.

Part 1 will survey this landscape and show how the fundamental *unity* of the Old and New Testaments—from shadow to fulfillment, type to reality—helps put many of these "offensive" passages in their proper perspective. How does "slaying the wicked" apply to me? How should we understand polygamy among God's people in Israel? Who is this God we are called to "fear"? This section will also reveal some of the unintended consequences of censoring the Scriptures—in our worship, ministry, and evangelism.

In part 2, we'll examine seven of the most frequently censored themes in the Bible and why an unashamed affirmation of these doctrines is needed for a healthy and fruitful faith. When we embrace the full character of God, for example, it actually deepens our understanding of the gospel and our fellowship with Christ. When God is big and we are small, we don't need to wear ourselves out on the treadmill of self-righteous reputation. We can cease our struggle to pretend and perform because we can rest in the righteousness of Christ. His grace becomes our refuge and we can cry out, with Paul, "I will boast all the more gladly of my weaknesses, so that the power of Christ may rest upon me" (2 Cor. 12:9).

When we censor the full character of God, we soften His justice, elevate man, and devalue our need for the cross. But when we embrace the entire Bible, we are freed from making God "fit" our politically correct, tame caricatures of a god who seems no more omnipotent than a divine grandpa. But like Aslan, God isn't safe. The Lion from the tribe of Judah has conquered. Eternally self-sufficient, He's dependent on no one. And His Word reveals His majesty and glory from Genesis to Revelation.

I've also included "A Final Word" with a discussion on where we go from here—daring to embrace the entire Bible—and how to identify our role in Jesus's mission to build His church (Matt. 16:18). This last section also gives some anchor-setting hope so that we might live out a healthy, balanced, and unashamed faith.

Whether you have unconsciously censored the Scriptures, as I have, or you have become increasingly aware of this widespread reality among many self-professing Christians, may you be recommitted to the whole counsel of God. May you take great delight in His Word (from beginning to end) and meditate on it day and night, that you might be like a fruit-bearing tree, planted by streams of water for God's glory and your joy (Ps. 1:2–3).

TALKING POINTS

American evangelicalism often presents a glowing presentation of the biblical text—highlighting well-loved favorites across radio waves and billboards—while leaving out those scriptural passages that might be offensive or embarrassing.

If the Bible is truly inspired by God and profitable for His people, then I should embrace the *whole* counsel of God for a healthy, balanced, and fruit-filled faith.

Maybe you've chased a feel-good faith by extracting those warm and fuzzy and socially acceptable Bible verses that we find plastered on bumper stickers and social media.

DISCUSSION QUESTIONS

1. As you have read the Bible, have you noticed a tendency to highlight or underline passages related to God's love and grace while hurrying through passages related to His justice and anger? What might that reveal about us?

2. Without looking ahead, what do you think are some of the most common "censored" texts in the Bible—passages that make Christians embarrassed? Why?

3. What are some advantages of embracing the entire Bible? Why would this be beneficial for you in your Christian walk?

2

AMERICA'S FIG-LEAF FAITH

According to a 2014 report, I live in the most "Bible-minded" city in America: Chattanooga, Tennessee[1]—a place where churches cover the land as the waters cover the sea. The local newspaper publishes daily Bible verses, and public schools have privately funded Bible classes. Local radio stations air a wide range of weekly sermons, and Christian music seems to rise above the city streets in a holy haze.

It's the Christian's garden of Eden ... or so it would seem.

Underneath the towering steeples and the "Jesus Saves" bill-boards, this little slice of Eden is not unlike other buckles of the Bible Belt across the American landscape. Even in cities such as New York and Los Angeles, Boston and Seattle, evangelical Christians (yes, evangelicals live there too!) boast of their strong commitment to the Word of God.

But this can be misleading because we use cultural morality or our own moral obedience like a fig leaf to hide our privately held embarrassment of certain portions *of* that Word. Let me explain.

ENTER SHAME

On the sixth day of creation, God created man in His image—male and female (Gen. 1:27). Genesis 2 describes how God made Adam from the dust of the ground and Eve from Adam's rib. In a comment oftentimes overlooked, the author added, "And the man and his wife were both naked and were not ashamed" (v. 25).

No sin, no competition, no shame. Adam and Eve enjoyed unbroken fellowship with God and with each other. Eve didn't have to fear the ridicule or rejection of Adam. Adam didn't have to question Eve's motives. They didn't have to say, "I'm sorry." Moreover, they enjoyed complete freedom to obey or disobey God; they didn't have the appetite for sin as you and I have had since birth.

Of the several commands that God gave them, only one carried an explicit consequence: "Of the tree of the knowledge of good and evil you shall not eat, for in the day that you eat of it you shall surely die" (Gen. 2:17). Before long, they found themselves staring at its fruit. It took only the suggestion of the serpent asking "Did God actually say?" to plant the seeds of doubt, of self-autonomy, and of independence from their Creator. In a moment, they wanted to be like God as the arbiters of good and evil, and so they ate the forbidden fruit.

What happened next was important: "Then the eyes of both were opened, and they knew that they were naked. And they sewed fig leaves together and made themselves loincloths" (Gen. 3:7). Rather odd, isn't it? Why did they sew fig leaves together, especially if it was just the two of them? It's not like the hyenas were going to start laughing.

They covered themselves because they were afraid of these new feelings called rejection and shame. As fallen, sinful humans, their natural instincts drove them to cover up, and man's proclivity to "cover up" has been the name of the shame game ever since. Today, many self-professing Christians are ashamed of certain portions of the Bible—whether they realize it or not—and use various "leaves" to cover up: morality, social justice, political activism, checklist obedience, or Yoga-inspired spirituality.

Censoring those embarrassing parts of the revelation of God reveals our own hidden shame. The apostle Peter may serve as a case in point. At times, Peter seemed like a champion of the Christian faith, affirming with confidence, "You are the Christ, the Son of the living God" (Matt. 16:16). And yet, when Jesus spoke of His own impending death, Peter took Him aside, rebuking Him: "Far be it from you, Lord! This shall never happen to you" (v. 22). Peter didn't want the King (or the King's men) to suffer—surely that wasn't God's will! But Jesus replied, "Get behind me, Satan!" Peter wasn't heeding the words of Jesus.

At another point, Peter pledged to stick by Jesus like a modern-day Promise Keeper: "I will not deny you!" (Matt. 26:35). But when the Romans began to mock, beat, and whip his Lord, Peter revealed his fear of rejection and persecution; he denied Jesus, and the rooster started to crow.

We're oftentimes like Peter when it comes to embracing and living out the words of our Lord—it simply costs too much. Our reputations, our jobs, and our lives are on the line. We've seen recently how some Christians have lost their jobs and have had to declare bankruptcy for calling sin *sin*. If the Christian life were about only earthly rewards, then it's certainly *not* worth it. But the beauty of the gospel is that we get something far greater than earthly reputation or a cushy job—we get God!

When I question, or *decide*, which passages in the Bible to follow, I miss out on the truth that sets me free. When we avoid the biblical practice of church discipline, for example, we miss out on the joy of seeing wayward sinners reclaimed or seeing Christ establishing greater peace and purity in His bride. When we avoid the doctrine of hell in our preaching and teaching, we miss the experience of gratitude of what we are saved *from* and the hope of what we are saved *for*.

Jesus didn't call us to a halfhearted, partially committed, self-empowering journey called "Christianity"; He called us to deny ourselves, take up His cross, and follow Him (Luke 9:23). This is nothing less than the electric chair for our flesh. We put to death our fear of man—to be accepted by the world—and return to a right fear of God, who didn't waste words when He gave us His Word. Jesus calls us into an upside-down kingdom, where we die to live, give up to gain, and worship a King who wore a crown of thorns, not gold. Embracing the entire Bible acknowledges Him as the everlasting author of truth, the Bulwark never failing.

THREE TYPES OF PICKERS

To use the metaphor of cherry-picking, we may identify three types of "pickers" who extract feel-good Bible verses while leaving behind the rest. First, there are liberal Christians who make man (or "human species" in certain politically correct circles) the measure of all things and reduce the Bible to some nice, moralistic exhortations—like a garnish around the main course of Gandhi, Mother Teresa, Buddha, or their favorite poet. Self-professing liberal Christians abandon the Christ of Scripture altogether *except* perhaps for His moral example to serve the poor and the outcast. However, while they may look to their 1990s bracelet and ask, "What would Jesus do?" they certainly wouldn't make a whip of cords and drive out the high rollers funding their political activism or tell a set-up prostitute, "From now on sin no more" (John 8:11). You see, even liberals cherry-pick the Scriptures.

A second type of cherry picker associates himself with evangelicalism but, ironically, refuses to affirm the whole counsel of God. He proclaims his *belief* in Scripture but his *dis*belief in certain portions of it. We see this schizophrenic faith played out in the public square by celebrity pastors.

Several years ago, a prominent megachurch evangelical pastor (now *ex*-pastor) who produced a popular video series and enjoyed bestseller status wrote an entire book challenging the existence of hell. For years, evangelicals flocked to sit at the feet of his preaching, teaching, and writing ministry. But his submarine secret finally breached the surface in 2011 with his attempt to erase hell in the name of love. With the sun at his back, he cruised out of the evangelical bay.

A third type of cherry picker might live closer to home: those who cherry-pick the Scriptures for a feel-good faith *without realizing they're doing it*. Here's where I must raise my hand and say, "Yep, that's me." This type of churchgoing, John 3:16–affirming picker is oftentimes "functionally embarrassed" by the Bible. We're not openly or blatantly embarrassed by Scripture, but we *functionally* reveal our embarrassment of the truth of the Bible by affirming, discussing, quoting, and preaching only certain passages while overlooking many others. Or we might have a subconscious angel on our shoulder telling us that something doesn't add up with how we handle the Bible, but we can't quite put our finger on it. Let me give you a couple of examples.

Some of these onward-Christian pickers march into cultural wars exploiting their unashamed condemnation of one or two social evils (such as homosexuality or abortion) to cover up their functional embarrassment of other offensive and seemingly archaic portions of the Bible (such as only men serving as pastors in the church). Others simply don't see the inconsistency. For example, what does a red-letter edition of the Bible *really* communicate? For many, it *subconsciously* communicates the lie that the words of Jesus are more important than other inspired words in the biblical text.

Several years ago, I was asked to speak at a conference for a church in Philadelphia. As I engaged in worship with their community, I noticed something rather unusual, at least to me. The people stood for the reading of the Bible out of respect and reverence for God's Word (which I loved!) *but only for readings from the Gospels.* When they read from an Old Testament passage or from one of Paul's epistles, they remained seated. Was it because Luke's account of the life of Jesus was "holier" than Genesis, a book that Jesus Himself considered inspired text? When I asked my host why we stood for only the gospel readings, he said he didn't know. It hadn't even crossed his mind.

Another example: Many evangelical Christians fight tooth and nail to have the Ten Commandments posted at courthouses and sanctuaries alike. That's fine with me. But beyond the question "Do you actually know the Ten Commandments?" is "What about the *fourth* commandment—keeping the Sabbath day holy?" You see, many who push hardest for the display of the Ten Commandments make no attempt to treat one day in seven as holy or set apart. Anything and everything fills the day like any other day of the week: mowing the grass, shopping, and football. While some Christians believe the fourth commandment was intended just for Israel or is now obsolete because we "rest" in Christ, the reality is that a Sabbath rest was actually instituted *before* the fall at creation. God wove a Sabbath rest into the very fabric of the created order.

How about you? Are there passages of Scripture you seem to avoid or skip over? Maybe it's time to examine your own heart and reclaim an affirmation of the whole counsel of God. As a "recovering picker" myself, I'm not suggesting that you join your local chapter of Pickers Anonymous (if there were such a thing). But I am suggesting that we take an honest evaluation of ourselves before God.

THE BLESSING OF EVALUATION

Imagine living in a "closed country" of the world where you didn't have access to a Bible. But one day you came across various *fragments* of the Bible that happened to be the very passages you would have otherwise (maybe unconsciously) ignored or censored.

Let's take Ephesians 6:5 to make this more tangible: "Slaves, obey your earthly masters with respect and fear, and with sincerity of heart, just as you would obey Christ" (NIV). Because of our troubled and sinful past as a nation, we are highly uncomfortable with this verse. But if this—and other passages like it—were all that you had of the Bible, how would you treat them? Would you cherish these fragments or toss them aside? Would they be as much of the "Word of God" as the rest of Scripture? What could you learn about yourself, about God's character, and about the Christian life from these seemingly obscure and offensive verses? How are we missing out?

In Deuteronomy 29:29, we read, "The secret things belong to the LORD our God, *but the things that are revealed belong to us* and to our children forever." That which God has revealed, every verse of Scripture, belongs to us and to our children forever. Rather than tucking them away, let's take a cue from the ancient monarch King Josiah.

During Josiah's reign in Judah, the high priest at the time, Hilkiah, found the Book of the Law in the temple. Yes, he *found* it! It had been lost and, therefore, completely neglected in the life of God's people. The secretary read God's Law to Josiah, and we're told, "When the king heard the words of the Book of the Law, he tore his clothes" (2 Kings 22:11). He was overwhelmed with guilt because of his sin and the sin of his people. Josiah and the people renewed their covenant with God, restored the Passover, and destroyed the idols of the land. After hearing God's *law*, Josiah "turned to the LORD with all his heart and with all his soul and with all his might" (23:25).

Why do I bring this up? The Book of the Law (the first five books of the Bible) includes many of the passages that might make us uncomfortable today: the global flood (Gen. 6–9), Lot sleeping with his daughters (Gen. 19), Judah sleeping with his daughter-in-law (Gen. 38), laws about slaves (Exod. 21), the command to drive out the Canaanites (Exod. 23), why Israel shouldn't eat camels (Lev. 11), the curses for disobedience (Lev. 26), the earth swallowing Korah (Num. 16), the talking donkey (Num. 22), God sovereignly choosing Israel (Deut. 7), and the stoning of rebellious children (Deut. 21).

When Josiah heard the Book of the Law, he was humbled and broken. If I spent time meditating on any one of these stories or commands, would I come to a place of brokenness and humility as Josiah did? Would you?

HALF-TRUTH CHRISTIANITY

When we preach, discuss, and selectively affirm only those portions of Scripture that make us feel happy and self-reliant—passages that you could gleefully present to your daughter's third-grade class—we miss out on a growing, healthy, and God-honoring faith.

My daughter loves the Berenstain Bears books, especially *The Forgiving Tree*. When we read before bed, she often reaches for this book. I open the cover and read, "For if you forgive men when they sin against you, your heavenly Father will also forgive you." Bring out the fuzzies! It's a wonderful quote from Matthew 6:14. But notice that the publisher left out the second part of Jesus's instruction: "But if you do not forgive others their sins, your Father will not forgive your sins" (v. 15 NIV). Ouch. You see, it's fine to rally around the glowing reminder that our heavenly Father forgives us when we sin, and we should! But we don't want the nagging reminder that if we don't (or won't!) forgive others, God won't forgive us. And so we hide behind the fig leaf of a half-truth.

Imagine a church that boasts of its massive missions program, complete with an annual conference featuring nationally recognized speakers and "real-life" missionaries. Banners and flyers announce it months in advance, and the church accountants begin tallying the projections for the next year's missions budget. Year after year, the congregation looks forward to the conference—to hear the chairman read the long roster of missionaries the church supports, how much is given toward global missions, and the feel-good faith of keeping the Great Commission. But this can be a fig leaf too.

Don't get me wrong. We are commanded to keep the Great Commission and make disciples of all nations (Matt. 28:19). But for *this* church, it can serve as a mask—a holy veil to hide behind— to cover up the many unbiblical (or biblically absent) aspects of their congregational life: the lack of church discipline, trading meaty sermons for entertaining skits, and ordaining an unqualified deacon simply because he can swing a hammer (try to find that in 1 Timothy 3). We become functionally ashamed of the Bible when we use morality or even a biblical command (such as the Great Commission) to hide our cherry-picking faith.

In 2013, the largest Presbyterian denomination in the United States voted *not* to include in their new hymnal the now-famous song "In Christ Alone" by Keith Getty and Stuart Townend. The nine-member Presbyterian Committee on Congregational Song voted to drop the hymn because the song mentions the fact that God's "wrath" was satisfied through the cross of Christ. They asked Getty and Townend if they would consider replacing those words with "The love of God was magnified," but the authors (thankfully) declined.

To put it bluntly, we don't want sin, wrath, or God's judgment in our Bibles. Richard Niebuhr, the early twentieth-century theologian, once remarked that we want a "God without wrath [who] brought men without sin into a kingdom without judgment through the ministrations of a Christ without a cross."[2] By censoring Scripture—functionally affirming only certain *portions* of the Bible—we end up creating a fictitious faith by making God in our image. We begin reinventing the whole story of creation, fall, and salvation to suit our fancies.

GUTTING THE GOSPEL

The apostle Paul asserted, "I did not shrink from declaring to you the whole counsel of God" (Acts 20:27). He preached Christ crucified from both easy and difficult texts of Scripture because he understood that—while the Holy Spirit led him to communicate God's revealed will (2 Pet. 1:21; 3:15–16)—*he* was not the arbiter of truth.

Paul's task was not to censor the Scriptures in hopes that people would be saved by hearing a *partial* gospel; his task was to preach the whole counsel of God because "faith comes from hearing, and hearing through the word of Christ" (Rom. 10:17). When we censor the Scriptures for a feel-good faith, we snub the authority of Christ. We "preach" what theologian Michael Horton has called "Christless Christianity."

Sometimes I wonder what my city would look like if Satan were in complete control. Rampant sexual immorality? Youngsters cursing old women? Animal sacrifices on Easter? Maybe. But picking up on an insight by Donald Barnhouse (longtime pastor of Tenth

Presbyterian Church in Philadelphia), Michael Horton speculated that if Satan took over a city, "all of the bars would be closed, pornography banished, and pristine streets would be filled with tidy pedestrians who smiled at each other. There would be no swearing. The children would say, 'Yes, sir' and 'No, ma'am,' and the churches would be full every Sunday … *where Christ is not preached.*"[3] You see, Satan's rule would be expressed in a church that is ashamed of the gospel.

Many of the most prominent preachers in America do not like talking about or using the word *sin*. They replace it with psychoanalytical words such as *troubles, anxieties,* or *brokenness.* But without sin, there is no Savior. There is no gospel. The reality of the *good news* of Jesus necessarily answers the *bad news* of the human condition. As soon as we begin censoring the Word, we undercut the Christ of the Word and, in effect, gut the gospel of its content and power.

YOU CAN DO IT. GOD CAN HELP.

A number of years ago, my wife and I bought a house in Atlanta—one that the real estate agent called a "handyman special." She told us that the "bones" were structurally sound; it just needed some TLC. With my handy-dandy DeWalt drill in one hand and a paintbrush in the other, I got to work. The daunting project, however, quickly became a fund-raising program for my local Home Depot. Despite my lack of carpentry and plumbing skills, I felt empowered by Home Depot's slogan, "You can do it. We can help." I kept telling myself, "I can do it!" My wife wasn't so sure.

It's a bad day, however, when the church begins taking its theology from a home-improvement store. I sometimes listen to sermons from TV preachers or skim through their *New York Times* bestsellers, and when I do, I seem to hear Home Depot's slogan in the back of my head, but with a twist: "*You* can do it. *God* can help."

The message in many of these sermons, books, and blogs is simple: *You* and *your* efforts can earn God's blessing. If you're in a pickle, just pull yourself out (what the Reformers might have called *sola boot-strapia!*). With a dash of God's help and a sprinkle of Dr. Phil, you can achieve anything! If you just have enough faith, God will reward you with health, wealth, and prosperity. That's right, friend (cough); no harm will come to you if you *really* believe in Jesus!

Try selling that to Jesus's disciples.

Home Depot Theology, simply put, is idolatry—magnifying the gifts of God above the Giver Himself. It's like the prodigal son wanting his father's possessions but not the father. In the end, the subtle "You can do it, God can help" message puts the positive spin of self-help in the place of Scripture, covering it up like a fig leaf.

But God is not our copilot. Jesus doesn't take the wheel when we hit a patch of ice. Our Lord isn't standing outside in the cold and rain just waiting for us to bring Him in. He's *El Shaddai*, "God Almighty," who lives and reigns as the sovereign and self-sufficient triune God of all eternity. He uses us in His mission on earth not because He *needs* us but because He *loves* us.

Maybe you're already convinced that all Scripture is God breathed and you feel no embarrassment about any portion of it. Or maybe the lights are turning on. Whether or not this is true of you, we are *all* prone to wander. We are *all* prone to leave the Word we love. Maybe we should ask the hard questions: Am I functionally embarrassed by the Bible? Do I avoid culturally offensive topics that the Scriptures address? Do I downplay God's holiness or judgment out of fear of what others might think of me? Do I use moral issues to cover my avoidance of undesired portions of Scripture?

The beauty of the gospel, however, is that our sin is no match for God's grace. Believer, if you've been guilty (as I have) of censoring the Scriptures, you can take rest in the promise that there is *now* no condemnation for those who are in Christ Jesus (Rom. 8:1). Take up your dwelling in the promises of God, humbly confess your sin, and thankfully receive His forgiveness. Maybe even search out those difficult passages and set up camp beside them. Ask God's Spirit to teach you new and wonderful things in His Word. And as the old hymn reminds us, "The things of this world will grow strangely dim in the light of His glory and grace."

TALKING POINTS

Censoring those embarrassing parts of the revelation of God reveals our own hidden shame.

The beauty of the gospel is that we get something far greater than earthly reputation or a cushy job—we get God!

By censoring Scripture—functionally affirming only certain *portions* of the Bible—we end up creating a fictitious faith by making God in our image.

DISCUSSION QUESTIONS

1. From the example in this chapter, imagine living in a closed country and all you had of the Scriptures was an (otherwise) offensive or "embarrassing" passage. How would you treat it? Would you cherish it as God's Word, or would you tuck it away? What could you learn about yourself, about God's character, and about the Christian life from these seemingly obscure and offensive verses?

2. What is the difference between affirming only parts of the Bible and inventing a completely new religion? Is there a difference?

3. What is the danger in believing a partial gospel? If there is good news, there must also be what?

3

BELIEVING GOD IN THE BIBLE

Mark Twain once quipped that a classic book is one that everyone wishes they have read but haven't.[1] John Bunyan's *The Pilgrim's Progress*, St. Augustine's *Confessions,* and John Calvin's *Institutes of the Christian Religion* might serve as good examples. It's one thing to actually read a book and quite another to drop into someone else's reading of it.

The Bible is a big book, and I would venture to say that most people—even most Christians—have never read it entirely. A true "classic," according to Twain's definition. Sure, we've read Bible verses on Twitter or from those Bible "salesmen" at baseball games flaunting verses on posters, banners, and bare chests. But most people have never invested the time into reading or studying the biblical text. But I'm not here to point fingers; I've been there too.

BELIEVING GOD

There's a big difference between believing *in* God and simply believing God. Most Americans will profess that they believe *in* God, which is about as patriotic as the back of our dollar bill. But as soon as we start talking about *who* God is or *what* He has said, that majority quickly splinters into hundreds (if not thousands) of disagreeing subgroups.

To be sure, this doesn't mean that all of those subgroups are equally true. The postmodern man is absolutely sure there are no absolutes. Absolutely. This, of course, is called relativism: what's true for you is true for you; what's true for me is true for me. But the more you attack the idea of absolute truth, the more it will attack you, because truth, by definition, is exclusive. Either Jesus rose from the dead or He didn't. Either He's the way, the truth, and the life or He's not. We need to strive to know the truth and believe the God of that truth.

While I was in seminary, I worked for a liberal denomination. It wasn't my first choice, but being a twenty-five-year-old who looked fourteen, with a résumé as long as a crab's nose, I didn't have many options. My first Sunday was the pastor's last Sunday, and for the next three years, I was the only pastoral staff. I preached on occasion, but the denomination filled most Sundays with its own pinch preachers who seemed much more interested in C. S. Lewis, Muhammad, and John Maxwell than Jesus.

After three years of ministry, I was burned out. Not only were my wife and I starving to be fed from God's Word, but we were also disillusioned about the church, the people, and my own calling to ministry. So I did what any self-respecting job seeker would do: I let Monster.com hook me up with a life insurance sales position.

Selling life insurance is a lot like making snow angels in the rain—it doesn't work. At least it didn't for me. After being licensed by the state of Alabama and enduring the company's strict training course, I felt like I could sell *anything*—you name it! Per their recommendation, I initially tried selling to my family. But to my astonishment, they politely smiled and said something like, "Yeah, maybe. We'll see. So when are you coming home for Christmas?"

The company had promised me "leads," which only *led* to cold calling and driving more than an hour in every direction to meet uninterested clients. Husbands demanded to know why I was calling their wives late at night, and elderly women just wanted to talk to a young man over the phone. However, the problem wasn't with the product; the problem was with me. I didn't *believe* in the product I was selling. In fact, I didn't even own life insurance myself!

It's tough to convince the world that the Bible is true when we don't communicate our own belief in it. When we are embarrassed by what it says or censor those "difficult" passages in sermons or in conversations on the elevator, we communicate as much. When we cherry-pick those feel-good verses and leave the convicting fruit behind, we rob God of His glory by making ourselves the arbiters of truth.

Deep down, censoring the Scriptures reveals our pride. We must decrease in humility and let God's Word increase in us, having confidence that the whole counsel of Scripture is sufficient. "Let the word of Christ dwell in you richly," Paul wrote (Col. 3:16).

Once we climb down from our high horse, we can treasure the true and living God with joy and delight. Like Zacchaeus in the sycamore tree, the wee little man must come down before the party can begin.

NATURAL AND SPECIAL REVELATION

God reveals Himself in both creation and the Bible. *Natural* revelation[2]—God's revelation in creation—testifies to His power, might, and wisdom (Rom. 1:19–20). "The heavens declare the glory of God, and the sky above proclaims his handiwork" (Ps. 19:1). When we study the ironic complexity of the simple cell, the "language" of DNA, or why sunsets are beautiful, we see something of the handiwork, wisdom, and power of God. Krispy Kreme doughnuts, it may be argued, are proof that God loves us.

But apart from the Bible—God's *special* revelation—we would not know that God exists in three persons: God the Father, God the Son, and God the Holy Spirit. We would not know God's plan of redemption or anything of the atoning work of Jesus on the cross. Furthermore, we would not know how we might love and obey God or of the realities of heaven and hell.

Both God's natural revelation and His special revelation testify to His existence, so that we might believe *in* Him. But holding fast to the whole counsel of God (Acts 20:27)—*believing Him*—takes an extra measure of faith. It moves us beyond censoring the Scriptures for a feel-good, man-made faith to humbly receiving a God-honoring, Spirit-wrought faith. I want to move beyond believing in God to actually believing God in His Word; and not just part of His Word—all of it.

THE BIBLE AS "GOD'S WORD"

Let's clear the air. I realize I am making a big assumption by claiming that the Bible is "God's Word." By saying that the Bible is "God's Word," I mean that God *inspired* chosen men to write the words God intended them to write, down to every letter and nuance. The early twentieth-century theologian Louis Berkhof said it this way:

> The Holy Spirit acted on the writers of the Bible in an organic way, in harmony with the laws of their own being, using them just as they were, with their character and temperament, their gifts and talents, their education and culture, their vocabulary and style. The Holy Spirit illumined their minds, aided their memory, prompted them to write, repressed the influence of sin on their writings, and guided them in the expression of their thoughts even to the choice of their words.[3]

Of course, the Bible also declares its own inspiration. The apostle Paul wrote, "All Scripture is breathed out by God" (2 Tim. 3:16). Peter, too, argued with reference to Scripture: "Men spoke from God as they were carried along by the Holy Spirit" (2 Pet. 1:21). And yes, God inspired *both* the Old Testament and the New Testament. Geerhardus Vos once wrote, "Whenever the New Testament speaks about the inspiration of the Old, it is always in the most absolute, comprehensive terms."[4] As we will explore a bit later, the Old Testament is just as inspired as the New Testament for Christians today.

That the Bible is "God's Word" conveys two necessary implications. First, because God is perfect and without error, His Word must also be perfect and without error. This means that Scripture (in its original manuscripts) is *inerrant*, free from all falsehood and mistake. While people have tried to argue successfully that the Bible contradicts itself or that it gives false scientific data, when these charges are examined closely, they fall flat (we'll look at some of these later).

The ultimate reason people do not want the Bible to be inerrant is because they do not want to answer to a just, holy, and sovereign God. In other words, we suppress the truth because we do not want to be held accountable (Rom. 1:18). Undercutting the inerrancy of Scripture, for many, has become the aim. As sinners, we can't stand the fact that we are not God but rather accountable to God.

Second, if the Bible is God's Word, it must be *authoritative*. God has all rights. He has complete authority over His creation as the sovereign Lord and King of the universe. He has every right to do all that honors Him and brings Him the most glory. He is not dependent on us or bound by us. Rather, God is completely free to work "all things according to the counsel of his will" (Eph. 1:11). This means that what He says—by way of His inspired text—carries the full weight of His authority. God does not conform to our wills; instead, we are transformed by the renewing of our minds according to the truth of His Word (Rom. 12:2).

A few years ago, I flew from Los Angeles to Sydney, Australia, to finish up some doctoral research. It's a long flight—nearly eighteen hours. If you've ever taken an overseas flight, you know that typically the seat in front of you has a video screen showing an animated airplane so you can follow the progress to its final destination. In my case, I watched that little plane *slowly* advancing over the vast Pacific. Lots of blue. Occasionally, I would see a little speck of land against the blue background of the screen and think, *If we went down, hopefully the plane would crash near an island so I could possibly swim for (or float to) safety. Hopefully before sharks ate me.* Believe me, I'm not typically a pessimistic guy.

When you're on an airplane for that length of time, you come to realize that you don't have much choice in the matter. You can't exactly turn the plane around or land it when you get uncomfortable. After ten hours, you've waved good-bye to comfort a long time ago. You have *some* room—maybe two inches—to move your knees, but that's about it.

After attempting to justify buying a voice-activated Star Wars R2-D2 from the *SkyMall* catalog for several hours, I decided to use my complimentary blanket to settle in for the rest of the trip.

Enter turbulence.

It felt as though King Kong had taken hold of the plane, trying to shake the passengers out like salt from a saltshaker. "Ladies and gentlemen, we've hit a patch of rough air. Please stay in your seats with your seat belts fastened." I looked at the flight attendant seated facing us, gripping her knees and wearing an expression of panicked tranquillity. At least the intercom voice had a pleasant Australian accent.

Rough air? I thought. I looked back at my screen, envisioning my *Cast Away* future. But I realized that I had little choice but to sit back, relax, and enjoy (okay, endure) the roller coaster. While I couldn't make the plane conform to my wishes at that moment, I *could* trust the pilot, the crew, and the flight plan.

God's Word is inspired, inerrant, and authoritative. Rather than attempting to shape it into something of my making, I am being molded and shaped by it. There are truths in the Bible that seem to shake me to the core, but it beckons my trust and confidence in a God who is using His Word to take me to His intended destination. As R. C. Sproul has said, "When there's something in the Word of God that I don't like, the problem is not with the Word of God, it's with me."

WHY THE NITTY-GRITTY MATTERS

America is finally waking up to the life-altering affects of what we eat. Never before have we witnessed such a multipronged campaign for organic, grass-fed, free-range, all-natural cuisine. When you need a PhD in Klingon to read the ingredients list for cheese puffs or Mountain Dew, you know we have a problem. The pictures of pink goo—called "meat"—and the mechanically separated beef fatty tissue have led consumers to value locally grown, organic food more than ever. While the "nutrition facts" and ingredients lists may be in *small* print, the nitty-gritty makes a *big* difference.

The Bible has well-known stories and lesser-known facts. Some portions are repeated over and over (such as the story of David and Goliath), while others seem to be completely ignored. Whether a text is popular and comforting or unpopular and convicting, every word is inspired, profitable, and a means by which God grows us in the faith.

When I took my first preaching class in seminary, the professor, Dr. Robert Smith, passed around the room a glass fishbowl containing small folded-up pieces of paper. Each sheet of paper had a biblical passage written on it, which contained one of the most "difficult" verses in the Bible to understand and, therefore, to preach on. It was the professor's way of throwing neophyte preachers into the deep end.

When I received the fishbowl, I reached my hand in and pulled out a piece of paper with "2 Kings 2:23–24" written on it. I didn't know those verses off the top of my head, so I turned there to read:

> [Elisha] went up from there to Bethel, and while he
> was going up on the way, some small boys came out
> of the city and jeered at him, saying, "Go up, you
> baldhead! Go up, you baldhead!" And he turned
> around, and when he saw them, he cursed them in
> the name of the LORD. And two she-bears came out
> of the woods and tore forty-two of the boys.

What? *She-bears* tearing forty-two boys? I wanted to quit. In all my years of going to Sunday school, I had never heard those verses. I didn't see *that* story painted on my children's ministry wall. I thought Elisha was a good guy, and it seemed (from the text) that God had honored his "cursing" of the young boys. Certainly some ancient scribe had made an error.

But the more I studied this passage, the more I came to realize how profound and instructive it was. When I studied these verses in their historical context, the meaning of the words used, and even the social customs (such as baldness), I understood that those boys were old enough to know what they were doing. They weren't just making fun of a bald man; they were attacking his calling as a prophet of God. They were provoking him to "go up" like his predecessor, Elijah, who "went up" in a whirlwind and chariots of fire (2 Kings 2:11). It was an unbelieving, sneering request of a repeat performance of Elijah's.

The young men's attack wasn't directed to Elisha so much as it was directed to God Himself. God had previously told Israel, "If you walk contrary to me and will not listen to me … I will let loose the wild beasts against you, which shall bereave you of your children" (Lev. 26:21–22). God was simply being true to His word.

Today, we want to believe in a God who is *only* loving. But God's love is just one of His many attributes. He is not *only* loving but *perfectly* loving … and just, holy, and sovereign. The verses in 2 Kings 2 show us a side of God that we do not consider enough. The character of God is more than nitty-gritty; it is true and essential for life, liberty, and happiness in Him.

As we read about those young men jeering at Elisha to "go up," we can hear the faint echo of crowds jeering at Jesus on the cross, "Come down. If you are really the Son of God, come down." As those boys experienced the bears' clawing and ripping as God's just judgment, so also did Jesus experience it all the more on our behalf. And there on the cross, where God's infinite love and justice collided, He paid our debt in full and cried out, "It is finished."

Oh, how I pray that we might proclaim the uncensored Scripture in all its fullness and grasp the *whole* counsel of God's Word. Then we will have joy and life in Him. May we not only believe in God but also believe Him and trust His holy Word. And may we come to realize that "man shall not live by bread alone, but by *every* word that comes from the mouth of God" (Matt. 4:4).

TALKING POINTS

It's tough to convince the world that the Bible is true when we don't communicate our own belief in it.

Krispy Kreme doughnuts, it may be argued, are proof that God loves us.

We suppress the truth because we do not want to be held accountable.

DISCUSSION QUESTIONS

1. What's the difference between believing *in* God and simply believing God?

2. If the Bible is "God's Word," what are the two necessary implications (as mentioned in this chapter)? Do you believe both of these things? Why or why not?

3. How does censoring the Scriptures reveal our pride?

4

WHY TRUST THE SCRIPTURES?

Over two billion people on the planet have at least *some* trust in the Bible. Either we are completely naive or there are some valid reasons for this high regard for God's Word. As we continue our exploration of the biblical censorship in America, we need to realize that Scripture is able to stand the test of careful scrutiny and skeptical analysis.

Many people, far more able and intelligent than I, have devoted their entire lives to the "defense" of the faith—a field of study called apologetics. While it is beyond the scope and purpose of this chapter to present any watertight arguments in detail, I do hope to whet your appetite for a deeper study into the many reasons to affirm the trustworthiness of the Bible.

The starting block might seem rather obvious, but we need to start with reading the Bible itself. Of course, we shouldn't read the Bible simply to get an *ichthus* plastered on our car bumpers or etch our names in the hall of faith—as if Elijah owes us a trip to heaven on his chariots of fire. Besides, that happened only once or twice.

On the contrary, we *should* read the Bible to know, love, and glorify God. The entire Bible—from "In the beginning" to "Amen"— sings of one overarching story, like a multipart ensemble supporting one another's voices in a unified oratorio. In it, we see God's manifold wisdom displayed as a multifaceted, beautiful tapestry of truth and love. No color is missing. No voice is flat.

That story centers on the eternal God, who is glorified by saving sinners through His Son and by His Spirit. We should read the Bible to know, love, and glorify God as well as know ourselves in relation to Him.

It's my hope that God will tune your heart to echo His song, to love and trust the entire Bible in all of its many parts, so that you will treasure God without censoring the Scriptures.

But before we look at how the Old and New Testaments fit together in this unified whole, it's important to say a word about *why* we should believe the Bible in the first place. If the Bible is full of errors, contradictions, and lies, then Christians are the most pitiful and gullible group of people on earth. But on the other hand, if the Bible is true in every detail, then we should stake our lives and eternity on its message.

THE EXTERNAL TESTIMONY OF THE BIBLE

The word *testimony* has various meanings—one being a proof or evidence supporting the reality of a proposition. We have many proofs and evidences supporting the trustworthiness of the Bible. These bear witness (give testimony) to the truth found therein. The *external* testimony of Scripture deals with the evidence of manuscripts and primary source documents that support the credibility of the biblical text.

The thirty-nine books of the Old Testament were written over a period of roughly fifteen hundred years. Originally penned in Hebrew and totaling only twenty-four books,[1] it was divided into three parts: the Law, the Prophets, and the Writings.

The New Testament assumes the existence of a *canon* (meaning "rule" or "measuring stick") as a body of truth called the "Scriptures" (Luke 24:27; John 5:39; Acts 17:2; 2 Tim. 3:14–16). In other words, the New Testament writers affirmed a collection of sacred writings, what we call the "Old Testament." But the New Testament also affirms itself as being inspired text.

Jesus, for example, emerged as one with divine authority. Note some of the ways in which He spoke of His own authority:

- "But I say to you" (Matt. 5:18, 22, 26, 28, 32, 34, 39, 44; 6:2, 16)—given in contrast and comparison to the words of Moses in the Law. In other words, Jesus's instruction was just as inspired as Moses's.
- "My words will not pass away" (Matt. 24:35; Luke 21:33). Imagine if your best friend said this. This is not normal.
- "All authority in heaven and on earth has been given to me" (Matt. 28:18). Sounds quite authoritative to me.
- "In many ways, God spoke to our fathers by the prophets, but in these last days he has spoken to us by his Son" (Heb. 1:1–2).

Add to this list the many claims of divinity by Jesus and His disciples.

This kind of authoritative teaching would naturally lead to an expansion of the Old Testament canon. Jesus's chosen apostles—those personally sent as His authoritative representatives—understood a "faith that was once for all delivered to the saints" (Jude v. 3). This is a contained collection of writings revealing what Jude called "the faith." Peter, too, recognized Paul's writings as "Scriptures," on par with the Old Testament (2 Pet. 3:16). Thus, the canon of Scripture is *closed* to further additions. We cannot add any more "revelation" or words to it (Rev. 22:18). That is why the Book of Mormon or the Book of Bob (or whoever) cannot be added to the canon of Scripture.

To be clear, the church did not *create* the list of biblical books; the church simply *recognized* them *as* Scripture. As New Testament scholar F. F. Bruce has argued, church councils did not confer on the twenty-seven books of the New Testament any authority they did not already possess but simply recorded their previously established canonicity.

What were the criteria for recognizing the New Testament canon? We may identify five in particular:

1. *Apostolicity*—written by or in the company of the apostles.
2. *Intrinsic authority*—makes authoritative and/or inspired truth claims.
3. *Consistent with Old Testament*—prophecies, fulfillment, references, and so on.[2]
4. *Evidenced power of God*—has transforming effect on lives (Heb. 4:12).

> 5. *Widely received by God's people*—the "received"
>   message (1 Thess. 2:13).

The New Testament books were circulated, acknowledged, and recognized as Scripture by the end of the first century. We had full canonical lists by the early 300s.[3]

What about the Apocrypha? The Roman Catholic Bible contains fourteen or fifteen books, called the Apocrypha, that are not included in most evangelical Bibles.[4] They are not included in our Bible because they were not in the Hebrew canon and the early Jewish authorities (such as Philo, Josephus, Council of Jamnia in AD 90) recognized them as *non*canonical. Moreover, Jesus and His apostles never accepted them as canonical[5] and the books make no claim to be of divine inspiration or authority. Even Jerome (347–420), who translated the "official" Bible of the Roman Catholic Church—the Latin Vulgate—argued that they should not be included. While the Apocryphal writings may encourage or edify the reader, they are not "inspired" biblical text.

There are more manuscripts of Homer's *Iliad* than any other book in ancient antiquity, 643 in total.[6] Except for the New Testament. Of the Greek New Testament manuscripts (about 5,700), only *one half of 1 percent* is in any question because of textual variants. Most of these can be easily solved by a simple omission error (absence of an "and" or plural form, and so forth). In *none* of these lines of the New Testament is the sense of the passage distorted or in question. Moreover, the early church fathers quoted the New Testament so extensively that it can be virtually reconstructed apart from the manuscripts altogether.

The sheer number of ancient manuscripts of the New Testament (over 25,000), of early translations from it, and of the various quotations of it in the oldest writings of the church is so large that it is practically certain that the true reading of every doubtful passage has been preserved. This is the academic field we call textual criticism, and neither liberal nor conservative scholars doubt the biblical text's authenticity. *Believing* it, however, is a different matter.

THE INTERNAL TESTIMONY OF THE BIBLE

Apart from the overwhelming evidence of the external testimony of Scripture, we also have solid *internal* testimony—the harmony of the biblical content itself. We can see this in three distinct ways.

Evidence 1: The Testimony of Jesus and the Apostles

Jesus claimed that the biblical message had divine authority (Matt. 4:4–10), was indestructible (Matt. 5:17–18), infallible (John 10:35), ultimately supreme (Matt. 15:3–6), factually inerrant (Matt. 22:29; John 17:17), and historically reliable (Matt. 12:40; 24:37–38).

What did Jesus think about Scripture? He believed it to be God's Word, inspired by the Holy Spirit. For example, when Jesus was teaching in the temple, He quoted Psalm 110, saying, "David himself, in the Holy Spirit, declared …" (Mark 12:36). You see, even though King David wrote Psalm 110, Jesus understood that he wrote *as he was carried along by the Holy Spirit*. In answering a question regarding divorce, Jesus quoted Genesis 2, noting that God "said" those Old Testament words (Matt. 19:3–6), even though they came from Moses. Jesus made thirty-eight direct appeals to "the law and the prophets" and said "it is written" (referring to the Old Testament) forty-six times.[7]

The apostles and New Testament writers routinely equated Scripture with what "God said" (see Gal. 3:8; Rom. 9:17), with reference to the Old Testament.[8] The point: Jesus, the apostles, and the biblical writers understood Scripture—written by the hand of men—to be ultimately the Word of God.

Evidence 2: The Honesty of Sin and Detailed Reports

Scripture does not try to cover up or censor the sins of the great saints of the Bible, nor does it omit striking detail. You would expect this if it were made up. If I were inventing a religion, I would not show its faults, especially the faults of its most famous adherents. But Scripture does this very thing.

For example, Abraham—the father of the faith—lied about his wife, Sarah, saying she was his sister (Gen. 12; 20). Moreover, he failed to trust God with having children in his old age (Gen. 16). Moses—the God-appointed leader who brought Israel out from slavery in Egypt—murdered a man (Exod. 2) and disobeyed God in the wilderness (Num. 20). David—the man after God's own heart— committed adultery with Bathsheba and had her husband killed (2 Sam. 11; see also Ps. 51). He also practiced polygamy, which was against God's command (1 Chron. 3; see also Deut. 17:17). Turning to the New Testament, we read about Saul—who later became Paul the apostle—overseeing the imprisonment and murder of numerous Christians (Acts 7–8; 22).

When we read the pages of Scripture, we are confronted with sheer honesty as recorded history. The Bible doesn't gloss over the sins of famous believers, nor does it try to hide its content by tucking it away somehow.

Scripture is also filled with such detail and historical precision that it would only be recorded as historical fact and eyewitness account. For example, the descriptions of the tabernacle, the conquest of Canaan, and the battles throughout the Old Testament are so detailed and observational that they can be read only as recorded history.

The dates, names, and places continue to enjoy archaeological support. Historical events marked down in Scripture can easily be verified through ongoing digs and discoveries, such as the Cyrus Cylinder. We shouldn't dismiss the significance of details. For example, after Jesus's resurrection, He appeared to seven of His disciples who were out fishing. They headed to shore, and John wrote:

> When they got out on land, they saw a charcoal fire in place, with fish laid out on it, and bread. Jesus said to them, "Bring some of the fish that you have just caught." So Simon Peter went aboard and hauled the net ashore, full of large fish, 153 of them. And although there were so many, the net was not torn. Jesus said to them, "Come and have breakfast." (John 21:9–12)

Notice the details: "large fish," "153 of them," and "the net was not torn." John was simply recording the event as history, not as a made-up story.

Evidence 3: Go See for Yourself

Much of the Bible is *prophecy*, which primarily means a "forth telling" from God through His chosen servants. It means to speak the Word of God, but it can also include the nuance of foretelling the future. More than 350 specific prophecies of Jesus Christ were fulfilled—twenty-four during the final twenty-four hours before His death. Even Jesus Himself claimed that He was fulfilling Old Testament scripture (Luke 4:16–21; John 13:18–19; Mark 14:26–28; Luke 22:36–37; 24:25–27).[9] Moreover, many crowds served as eyewitnesses to Jesus (Matt. 9:1–8; 14:13–21; Mark 1:29–34; 2:1–12; 3:7).

But probably the most remarkable testimony came from the eyewitnesses of Jesus's resurrection from the dead. In his first letter to the Corinthian church, Paul wrote:

> For I delivered to you as of first importance what I also received: that Christ died for our sins in accordance with the Scriptures, that he was buried, that he was raised on the third day in accordance with the Scriptures, and that he appeared to Cephas, then to the twelve. Then he appeared to more than five hundred brothers at one time, *most of whom are still alive.* (1 Cor. 15:3–6)

In other words, go ask them yourself! If what Paul said was untrue, any one of those eyewitnesses could have easily disproved the message of the resurrection. The early spread of Christianity would have come to an immediate halt. But this was not the case. We see here a community witness to both the fulfillment of Old Testament prophecy and Jesus's miracles by those who could verify their validity and reliability.

THE EXPERIENTIAL TESTIMONY OF THE BIBLE

Several years ago, I was asked to teach a "Bible Institute" at a local church—a four-week intensive course that focused on why I believe the Bible in an unbelieving world. In addition to the manuscript evidence and the internal testimony of biblical harmony, I also pointed out ten *experiential* reasons why I believe the Bible to be true. In other words, when I observe the world around me and honestly examine the inclinations of my own heart, they dovetail and harmonize with what I see in Scripture. Here they are, in no particular order:

> 1. **Our sense of morality and justice over wrongs committed.** Humanity has a deep sense of right and wrong. Murdering a young girl makes us cringe in disgust. Why? The Bible gives valid reasons for this. For one, we were created in the image of God (Gen. 1:27), bearing an innate moral compass from which to differentiate right and wrong. Sure, people continually suppress this reality, but we all know it exists. This is why even atheists today are trying, *in vain*, to explain the reality of morality according to their faith (yes, faith) system.[10]

2. **Our need for intimacy, relationship, and community.** Why is solitary confinement in prison so horrible? Why do we all want to be known and loved? Why is the number-one fear among many people rejection and loneliness? It's because we were created for relationship—and that is because we were created in the image of a God who *is* community in the Trinity (Father, Son, and Holy Spirit). Not only does God experience perfect community, but the Creator has also entered into relationship with His creation. We are made in the image of a relational God. Thus, we long to be known and loved and, as St. Augustine once prayed, "Our hearts are restless until they find rest in Thee."

3. **Our sense of human rights and dignity.** Closely related to our sense of morality is our sense of human worth and dignity. If we simply evolved from some primordial goo when the rain fell on the rocks for billions of years and eventually came alive, then there can be no consistent human value. I worked for a human rights organization in London, England, and encountered some of the most horrific treatment of people on earth. Except for those select individuals who are the perpetrators of the crimes, everybody innately detests human

rights violations in which a person's dignity is trampled.

4. **Our hope in spite of pain and suffering.** Our existence as humans is not a "foundation of unyielding despair," as one atheist put it.[11] Suffering is meaninglessness *apart* from the biblical message. We see many passages in Scripture showing how God uses suffering in hundreds of ways: from punishing sin to sanctifying His people, from weaning us from a love of this world to bringing Himself the most glory. Every affliction is meaningful, though we may not know what that meaning is in the immediate context. Only Scripture provides consistent and meaningful answers to the reality of suffering and evil in the world (we'll look at this more in detail later).

5. **Our desire for and acknowledgment of truth, which cannot be denied.** Why is it that we desire to know the truth? Whether we take the red pill or the blue pill, we all want to know what's real. In fact, we can't even deny its existence. Try denying absolute truth. It doesn't work because you end up proving that which you try to deny. Jesus is the way, the truth, and the life. He makes reasonable statements and propositions—truth claims. Though these truth claims require the element of faith, they

harmonize with our propensity to seek truth, a propensity I witness every day.

6. **Our desire to worship something beyond ourselves.** Whether it's an actual object of worship, such as a man-made idol, or simply an ideal that we chase, such as the American Dream, we all desire to worship something bigger, greater, and beyond ourselves. Oftentimes it's the ideal of ourselves—loving ourselves for what we hope we will be rather than for what we are. But why? Scripture provides the answer: Because we have a God-sized hole in our hearts. We were made to worship. However, sin twists our hearts—as John Calvin would say—into idol factories. Instead of worshipping the true and living God, we turn anything and everything into objects of worship.

7. **The presence and reality of sin, even among children.** You can't deny the fact that something is terribly wrong with humanity. When I am honest, my heart is full of sin, envy, and pride. This didn't appear suddenly when I became an adult. When you tell a two-year-old, "Don't touch that wet paint!" the little hand splats on the wall. Rebellion is the name of the human-nature game. And it's been that way since the fall of Adam and Eve in Genesis 3.

8. **Natural revelation and the *lesser* faith of intelligent design.** The reality and presence of love and self-sacrifice reverse evolutionary theory. We'll look at the issue of creation later on, but if we live in a world in which the strong eat the weak, what do we make of the strong sacrificing *for* the weak? The gospel says that the strongest One in the universe laid down His own life for those who could not save themselves, the weak. The freedom won by this act—on behalf of the weak—empowers them to go and do the same. And I've seen this selfless love over and over again. In this way (and thousands more like it), the truth of God's creation takes a *lesser* faith than natural evolution.

9. **Provides a source of purpose and meaning.** What is the purpose of life? Why are you here on earth? Most people would say, "To be happy." But think about it. Is that the end of your existence? Is that why you are really here? Everything in me longs for a sense of purpose and meaning. You might say that I'm being naive. But you, too, desire to live for something more than jelly doughnuts (even if they make you happy).

10. **The countless number of people, like me, who have been transformed by the grace**

of God. Is it just a fluke that billions of people throughout history have a shared experience in the gospel of Jesus Christ? I find it rather interesting when government leaders, school officials, and Islamic radicals try to ostracize and outlaw Christian influence. Why is our government so scared of Christians? Is it because Christians are terrorizing schools and airports with bomb threats and hijacking? Of course not. Is it because Christians are unusually cruel like Hitler, Stalin, or Pol Pot? No, they all hated God. It's because the biblical message *itself* has proved powerful to change lives. And the militant atheist, agnostic, or any other unbeliever cannot handle the spread of a truth he's trying to suppress. God has won my heart, mind, soul, and strength. Even though I sin and oftentimes fall in my Christian walk, my love for God remains because He first loved me.

THE WORK OF THE HOLY SPIRIT

In the final analysis, however, we believe the Bible to be God's Word *not* ultimately by the mountain of historical, textual, archaeological, eyewitness, and experiential evidence, but by the work of the Holy Spirit. In what is probably the best statement on Scripture as being the Word of God, the Westminster Larger Catechism (1647) states:

> The Scriptures manifest themselves to be the Word of God, by their majesty and purity; by the consent of all the parts, and the scope of the whole, which is to give glory to God; by their light and power to convince and convert sinners, to comfort and build up believers unto salvation: but the Spirit of God bearing witness by and with the Scriptures in the heart of man, is *alone able fully to persuade it* that they are the very Word of God. (Q4, emphasis added)

Read that again carefully. While Scripture provides a multitude of reasons for us to trust it as the Word of God, the Holy Spirit is the only One who brings that truth home.

When we censor the Scriptures, we communicate our *dis*trust of God's Word. But my hope is that you will find freedom in believing the whole counsel of God. It is reliable, accurate, and trustworthy, and seeing the fundamental unity of Scripture helps us explain many of the "difficult" passages we encounter, which we will look at next.

TALKING POINTS

The entire Bible—from "In the beginning" to "Amen"—sings of one over-arching story, like a multipart ensemble supporting one another's voices in a unified oratorio.

In the Bible, we see God's manifold wisdom displayed as a multifaceted, beautiful tapestry of truth and love.

Scripture does not try to cover up the sins of the great saints of the Bible, nor does it omit striking detail.

DISCUSSION QUESTIONS

1. If the Bible is full of errors, contradictions, and lies, then how are Christians the most pitiful group of people on earth? On the other hand, if the Bible is true in every detail, then what should be our response to its message?

2. What do we mean by the "external," "internal," and "experiential" testimonies of Scripture?

3. In addition to the ten mentioned in this chapter, can you think of other experiential reasons that affirm the message and truth of the Bible?

5

STONING THE ADULTERER: THE UNITY OF SCRIPTURE

If you flip through the Bible for any length of time, you will probably encounter some rather strange and harsh stories. In many instances, we find God commanding His own people, Israel, to do some terrible things—or at least it seems that way from our perspective. We also find commands that seem to fit the cruel-and-unusual category of contemporary law. For example, if a son dishonored his parents, all the men of the city were to stone him to death (Deut. 21:18–21). The same penalty applied to an adulterer (Lev. 20:10) and a Sabbath breaker (Num. 15:32–36).

The God of the Old Testament seems, from a quick glance, to be quite different in character from the God of the New Testament. While the God of the Old Testament seems cruel, vindictive, wrathful, and outright unjust (one might say), the God of the New Testament is gracious and loving, as seen in the example of Jesus of Nazareth, who loved prostitutes and ate with tax collectors and sinners.

This raises the question: Does the Bible have an essential unity? In other words, how do the two Testaments fit together without compromising the essential integrity of the whole? Related to these questions is: Why don't Christians today stone adulterers or disobedient children if those commands are found in the Bible? Why do Christians eat barbecue and shrimp without a second thought (Lev. 11:7, 10)?

I have atheist friends who ask these exact questions. Answering these questions is not easy, but we don't need to run away, and we don't need to censor the Scriptures. Understanding the essential unity of Scripture—as well as the various points of *dis*unity—helps shed light on some of these difficult shadows.

CONTEXT, CONTEXT, CONTEXT

Journalists and political pundits often accuse Christians of being inconsistent: obeying parts of Scripture while ignoring others. Tim Keller, bestselling author and a pastor in New York City, has argued that such an accusation is not exactly fair and balanced. He wrote:

> I don't expect everyone to understand that the whole Bible is about Jesus and God's plan to redeem his people, but I vainly hope that one day someone will access their common sense (or at least talk to an informed theological adviser) before leveling the charge of inconsistency.[1]

One of the key reasons Christians *seem* to be inconsistent is because those who are unfamiliar with the Bible may not understand how to properly read the Scriptures nor the importance of biblical *context*. Essentially, context involves the various historical circumstances and literary information that surround a particular text or event. It provides the setting, presents a framework, and guides the reader on *how* to accurately interpret a biblical passage.

If you've ever looked for a new home, your real estate agent probably told you, "Location, location, location." Why? Because the location of the home determines the price, local resources, school options, and even the potential for crime. Context works similarly. If you don't pay attention to the context of a biblical passage, it could land you in a place completely foreign—where you begin making inappropriate and inconsistent applications to your daily life. Let me explain.

Did you know that the Bible says, "There is no God" (Ps. 14:1)? There you have it. It's right there in the text. If you were to take that statement apart from the words found immediately before them— "The fool says in his heart"—you would conclude that the Bible is completely inconsistent. But the context helps you understand the text: only a fool would suppress the truth and reality of God.

I oftentimes see Jeremiah 29:11 plastered on billboards, read at weddings, and whispered to those filing for bankruptcy. It reads, "'For I know the plans I have for you,' declares the LORD, 'plans to prosper you and not to harm you, plans to give you hope and a future'" (NIV). Who wouldn't want that displayed for all to see? Great verse.

But if you miss the context of Jeremiah—namely, that it was written to God's people during a time of suffering and exile—you might come up with all sorts of baseless applications to your own life. Hitler, for example, could have read this and said, "Sweet! God has a great plan for me … for prosperity and hope! Away with the Jews!" Or I could read it and make the inappropriate application that I have a future and hope in the NBA with a multimillion-dollar contract. I mean, the verse mentions prosperity. Notwithstanding the fact that my earlier dreams in the NBA didn't quite reach the rim after I tried out *twice* for the JV basketball team in high school, I could come to some very wrong conclusions.

Sometimes, Christians will complain that they faithfully followed the Bible verse "Train up a child in the way he should go; even when he is old he will not depart from it" (Prov. 22:6) but their children *have* gone astray! They *have* departed from it. Did God lie? Did He fail to keep His promise? Of course not. It's when you realize that the book of Proverbs is wisdom literature—written for a path of wise living—that the passage makes sense. We are not to treat it like a magical formula of cause and effect. Just because you put in A (training up a child in the way he should go) doesn't mean that you automatically get B (a lifelong Christian). Besides, we are to plant and water the gospel in the hearts of our children, and it is "*God* who gives the growth" (1 Cor. 3:7). It is *wise* (and obedient) to bring up a child in the way he should go, and if you do that, he *usually* will not depart from it. It's not a promise of reward; it's godly wisdom for the way.

By far the most popular passage I see taken out of context is Philippians 4:13, which reads, "I can do all things through him who strengthens me." But we must ask: Who is the "I," what are the "all things," and how does God "strengthen" a person? When you look at the previous verse, the context, you see that the apostle Paul was talking about how he had lived in both poverty and plenty. He had enjoyed times of abundance, and he had faced hunger and need. But whatever his lot, he could say, with the hymnist, "It is well with my soul." He believed that God strengthened him to live for Christ in every situation, in all things, even in times of affliction.

"I can do all things through him who strengthens me" *doesn't* mean that you should try swimming across the Atlantic Ocean while repeating the verse over and over to yourself. But you *could* draw an appropriate application when you have suffered a loss—financially or from the death of a family member. God sustains and strengthens those who trust in Him, cast their burdens on Him, and take up their lodgings in the promise of eternal life through Jesus Christ our Lord.

Both the *words* of the Bible and the *circumstances* in which they were written have great significance. The occasions and even the biblical writers themselves provide the context for the words. The Bible is God's Word, but He used real people in real history to record His self-revelation. Understanding the context of any Scripture passage is vitally important to understanding the passage itself.

Historical Context

When you come to a Bible verse, especially one that might be difficult to understand, you need to note at least three types of contexts. The first type is the *historical* context. Why did the author write the book? What was the occasion? When did he write it?

In 1 John, for example, the apostle John taught: "[Jesus] is the propitiation for our sins, and not for ours only but also for the sins of the whole world" (2:2). If you have ever read John 10 or Ephesians 5, you might think that these passages are inconsistent, especially if you are of the Reformed persuasion. Either Jesus actually died to atone for the sins of every single person in the world—as the passage in 1 John seems to suggest—or He died *solely* for His "sheep," His "bride," the church.

It's only when we realize that John was writing in a Jewish context that we come to see that there is no contradiction. Jesus (a Jew) didn't die just for Jews, the chosen people we find in the Old Testament. He died for everybody—including Jews, Greeks, Chinese, Americans, and Antarcticans. That doesn't mean that He died for every single individual; it means that Jesus "ransomed people for God *from* every tribe and people and language and nation" (Rev. 5:9). Understanding the historical context is vital to understanding the biblical text. A good study Bible can help immensely with this.[2]

Literary Context

Second, it's important to understand the *literary* context. The Bible contains many different types of literature—poetry, epistle, historical narrative (to name a few). It also contains metaphors, similes, parallelism, imagery, typology, allegory, and repetition. It also contains repetition. Psalm 23:1 tells us, "The LORD is my shepherd; I shall not want." It's a metaphor to show *how* God takes care of His people, who are like sheep—needy, wandering, hungry, and oftentimes dumb. In Psalm 18:2, King David wrote, "The LORD is my rock and my fortress." God isn't an actual rock, of course, but He *is* strong and immovable like a large boulder.

These sorts of metaphors are fairly easy to discern. Other passages in Scripture, however, are more difficult and take extra care and attention. For example, Genesis 1 speaks of six "days" of creation. Is Genesis 1 poetry or epistle, or is it written as actual history? We will explore this later in more detail (I'll hold you in suspense), but how you read it—its literary genre—has a profound impact on how you interpret the text.

Redemptive Context

Third, we need to understand the *redemptive* context. How does a particular text fit into the whole story of redemption? Immediately after Adam and Eve "fell" into sin in the garden of Eden (Gen. 3), God told Satan, "I will put enmity between you and [Eve], and between your offspring and her offspring; he shall bruise your head, and you shall bruise his heel" (v. 15). Who is the One who would eventually come from woman and crush the power of Satan?

Understanding this verse in the story of redemptive history points us to Christ, who was born of the Virgin Mary, lived a sinless life, suffered on the cross, and triumphed over the grave when He was raised to life. It points us to a time to come when "at the name of Jesus every knee should bow, in heaven and on earth and under the earth, and every tongue confess that Jesus Christ is Lord, to the glory of God the Father" (Phil. 2:10–11). From beginning to end, the Bible presents a unified story of God's passion for His own glory, as seen in the redemption of sinners wrought through the work of His Son, Jesus Christ.[3]

JESUS IN THE OLD TESTAMENT

When we read about the great "saints" of old—Abraham, Isaac, and Jacob—or tragic events that took place during Old Testament times (e.g., war, rape, or slavery), we need to lift our eyes up to see the redemptive context, in which the Son begins to rise above the dark horizon. We will look at some of these more difficult subjects in part 2, as they point to the need of restoration and redemption found in Christ.

When you read Scripture in this way, you begin to see, for example, that Jesus is the truer and greater Joshua who leads us into the Promised Land of fellowship with Him and in fellowship with the great cloud of witnesses forever. Christ is the truer and greater David who reigns as the sinless King of Kings and Lord of Lords (1 Tim. 6:15). As the prophets of old spoke God's Word to the people, so Jesus—the eternal Word—became flesh and dwelled among the people (John 1:14). As the priests of the Old Testament sacrificed animals on behalf of the people, so Christ became the Lamb of God as the once-for-all sacrifice for sinners (1 Cor. 5:7).

When Jesus was walking on the road to Emmaus, after His death and resurrection, He encountered two confused travelers (Luke 24). These men were hoping for a king and savior to deliver them from Roman rule, and they couldn't understand why Jesus, who they had hoped would fulfill this role, had died. After probing their confused state, Jesus said, "O foolish ones, and slow of heart to believe all that the prophets have spoken! Was it not necessary that the Christ should suffer these things and enter into his glory?" Luke added, "And beginning with Moses and all the Prophets, he interpreted to them *in all the Scriptures* the things concerning himself" (vv. 25–27).

What were the "Scriptures" in their context? Our Old Testament. You see, the entire Old Testament points to Jesus. When you observe tragedy or evil in the book of Job or the story of Samson (Judg. 13–16), it cries out for redemption, for healing, and for restoration. Christ would bring all three. He would enter into a context of affliction, pain, and evil and become "obedient to the point of death, even death on a cross" (Phil. 2:8). Understanding the big-picture history of redemption helps us to understand the meaning of particular texts.

I'm a pastor and people often wonder what I *do* on the other six days of the week, as if I head to the beach and work on my tan until Sunday. But it's a fair question. As is the case with most pastors I know, it's not uncommon to put in sixty-plus hours because our time is often shaped around other people's schedules, problems, and illnesses. We have worship planning, sermon preparation, counseling, visitations, lunch appointments, staff meetings, website maintenance, vision casting, funerals, weddings, event planning, new members' classes, Sunday school, mercy ministry, and outreach. We lead Bible studies, small groups, and review books from parishioners. Last week, I even chased a chipmunk out of the sanctuary. Somehow, I missed the chipmunk-chasing class in seminary!

I also find myself listening. Some older folks in our congregation are lonely and simply want somebody to talk to. Others are not lonely; they just like talking. One member, Steve (not his real name), is plagued with a chronic need to tell stories—*long* stories. And his stories are like God's mercies: they're new every morning. Strangely, his stories also fit together, day after day. If I miss a particular day's story or forget something he's said, the overarching, multiday story can become very confusing.

The Bible has an overarching story centered on the person and work of Jesus Christ. Some parts of the story may be very confusing, but when you consider the historical, literary, and redemptive contexts, they begin to come together and make sense.

THE UNITY OF SCRIPTURE

One of the most helpful and faithful ways to see the overarching unity of Scripture is through the lens of the various biblical *covenants*. (If you are a die-hard dispensationalist, don't put the book down yet. There's something here you need to consider.) A biblical covenant is a bound, committed relationship between God and His people.[4] It contains promises and obligations, blessings and curses.

Throughout Scripture, we see a number of covenants. In the beginning, God made a covenant with Adam in the garden.[5] It was a bound relationship with obligations. The terms were simple: obey God by not eating of the forbidden fruit (Gen. 2:17). The covenant also had consequences: If you do eat of the forbidden fruit, you will surely die. Obedience brought life; disobedience brought death.

Adam didn't have a sin nature like you and I do. He was completely free to obey or disobey. But as we know, through the temptations of Satan and the lure of his bride, Adam disobeyed and fell into sin. This covenant—oftentimes called the covenant of works—is important to understanding the unfolding story of salvation in Christ. The apostle Paul said that the "first Adam" brought death while the "last Adam," Jesus, brought life (1 Cor. 15:42–49;

Rom. 5:12–21). Adam was our representative (federal) head; when he fell in sin, so did we. That's why we are prone to sin and rebellion, even from the womb.

In His divine justice, did God simply forget the whole creation and humanity idea? Not a chance. He entered into a covenant of *grace*. He would have been completely just to kill everybody immediately. But He didn't. He offered grace, His unmerited favor. We see His covenant of grace promised right there in the curses of the fall (Gen. 3:15). We see it demonstrated with the salvation of Noah and his family (Gen. 6–9). We see it when God first called out a people to be His treasured possession, with Abraham (Gen. 12–17). We see this covenant of grace when God led His people out of Egypt, from slavery and bondage, through His servant Moses (Exod. 19–24). We see it displayed with promise of the eternal throne of King David's lineage (2 Sam. 7). And we see it promised with the "new covenant" through the prophet Jeremiah (Jer. 31).

On the night when Jesus was betrayed—just before His arrest and subsequent crucifixion—He instituted the Lord's Supper. The bread symbolized His body, broken for sinners. The cup symbolized His blood, poured out for sinners. Jesus said, "This cup is the new covenant in my blood" (1 Cor. 11:25). On the cross, Jesus would pay the penalty of our covenant breaking. "With his wounds we are healed ... The LORD has laid on him the iniquity of us all" (Isa. 53:5–6).

All of these covenants—and they're called "covenants"—are linked together in a progressive, organic relationship. They are connected by the sovereign grace of God. Instead of wiping rebellious humanity from the face of the earth once and for all when Adam sinned, He showed grace. God sent His only Son into this world to live a perfect, sinless life for His bride and to die under the full measure of God's just wrath for sin. This is the gospel. "For our sake he made him to be sin who knew no sin, so that in him we might become the righteousness of God" (2 Cor. 5:21).

Today, we can enjoy a covenantal, bound relationship with God. We are *His* people and He is *our* God only because Jesus has become our great Covenant Keeper, living for us the life we should have lived and paying the ultimate price for our covenant breaking, the wages of sin.

Here, we see the fundamental unity of Scripture. God would meet our obligations and requirements of the covenant through His Son. *Jesus has accomplished for you everything that God has required of you, for your salvation.* And God would remain perfectly just in doing so because His love for us and His wrath against sin collided on the cross of our Lord. That is why Paul wrote, "That [God] might be just and the justifier of the one who has faith in Jesus" (Rom. 3:26).

THE DISCONTINUITY OF SCRIPTURE

While there is certainly a fundamental unity of Scripture, we shouldn't mask some of the elements of *dis*continuity. In fact, the reason we have an *Old* Testament and *New* Testament reflects this reality.[6] While there are several different aspects of discontinuity, we'll focus our attention on only one for the purposes of this book: the temporary nature of the covenant with and laws of Moses.

The first five books of the Bible—Genesis, Exodus, Leviticus, Numbers, and Deuteronomy—are often called the Five Books of

Moses, the Law of Moses, the Pentateuch, or the Torah (Hebrew for "law"). They contain the historical accounts of the patriarchs of Israel, the exodus out of Egypt, and the various laws to govern the worship and theocracy of the nation of Israel. These include: dietary laws, judicial laws, ceremonial laws, sexual laws, sacrificial laws, property laws, civil laws, and moral laws (such as the Ten Commandments). Most of the "crazy and cruel" laws that atheists, agnostics, and skeptics criticize come from these books. And the laws found in these books might even embarrass many Christians, at least initially.

It's important to remember that God gave these commands to Moses *before* Israel entered the Promised Land, Canaan, and set up their permanent society. If the people obeyed these laws, they would experience blessing and it would go well with them as they entered and established the land. But if they disobeyed these laws, they would experience God's curse, suffering, and even exile (Lev. 26; Deut. 28). If you have studied Old Testament history, you know that they disobeyed God and, thus, suffered the curses of the Mosaic covenant.

When Jesus came, the old wineskins of the Mosaic covenant, with its laws for the theocracy of the nation of Israel, couldn't contain the new wine He brought (Mark 2:22). The people of God would no longer be confined to the nation of Israel but would include the Gentiles as well, just as the Old Testament promised (Gen. 12:3; Isa. 42:6; 49:6; Joel 2:28). Through His death, Jesus has broken down the dividing wall of hostility between Jew and Gentile, creating one new people in Himself (Eph. 2:14–15). This is the church, the "Israel of God" (Gal. 6:16).

But rather than simply abolishing the Old Testament laws, Christ *fulfilled* them (Matt. 5:17). Again, we see the unity of Scripture. The Law of Moses was given "*until* the offspring [Christ] should come to whom the promise had been made" (Gal. 3:19). The judicial, ceremonial, dietary, and civil laws of Israel would find their end in the person and work of Jesus Christ. The old covenant that included these theocratic laws has been abrogated by the new covenant in Him. That was why the writer of Hebrews said, "In speaking of a new covenant, he makes the first one obsolete" (Heb. 8:13).

Thus, Christians do not stone adulterers (Matt. 5:38–48; John 8:1–11). The church is not to wield the sword of justice; that's the responsibility of the civil government (Rom. 13:1–7). Christians are free to eat barbecue, meat, and other foods previously forbidden (Acts 10:12–15) because we are made clean, not by diet, but through the Spirit of Christ. The veil of the laws of Moses has been removed:

> For to this day, when they read the old covenant, that same veil remains unlifted, because only through Christ is it taken away. Yes, to this day whenever Moses is read a veil lies over their hearts. But when one turns to the Lord, the veil is removed. Now the Lord is the Spirit, and where the Spirit of the Lord is, there is freedom. (2 Cor. 3:14–17)

While the old covenant community's worship was centered in Jerusalem, the new covenant community's worship is *de*centralized.

Why? Because Christ has become the sacrificial Lamb on behalf of His people from all nations and is the only Mediator between God and man (1 Tim. 2:5). Jesus told the Samaritan woman at the well, "Woman, believe me, the hour is coming when neither on this mountain nor in Jerusalem will you worship the Father.… God is spirit, and those who worship him must worship in spirit and truth" (John 4:21, 24).

To be sure, *both* Old Testament believers *and* New Testament believers were saved through faith and not by works (Gen. 15:6; Rom. 4). Christians, too, are "sons of Abraham" by faith (Gal. 3:7). Again, we see the continuity and unity of Scripture. But while the nation of Israel was set apart from the surrounding nations by faithfully obeying the various laws of Moses, Christians (made up of converted Jews and Gentiles alike) are set apart as holy through faith in Christ, which is expressed in obedience to the "law of Christ" (Gal. 6:2).

THE TEN COMMANDMENTS

One last comment before we conclude. The Ten Commandments (Exod. 20; Deut. 5) fall into a unique category. Yes, they were given with these other laws for the nation of Israel, but they uniquely express the *moral* intent and character of God, which is timeless. Thus, they are often called the "moral law."

Jesus affirmed the Ten Commandments throughout His ministry and incorporated them into the law of Christ. In fact, He extended their application so that murder wasn't only the outward act but also included the inward anger toward your brother. Adultery wasn't only the act of sleeping with another man's wife but also the inward lust of the heart. While some may think that Jesus came and eased the commandments of old, He actually heightened and strengthened them. The bottom line, He said, was, "You therefore must be perfect, as your heavenly Father is perfect" (Matt. 5:48). To which we respond, "How can *anybody* be saved?" Answer: "What is impossible with man is possible with God" (Luke 18:27).

No one is saved through keeping God's laws. Rather, we are saved through faith alone in the One who has kept God's laws *for us*. We are counted righteous in God's sight because of Christ's obedience credited to our accounts. As those who are justified and adopted into God's family, we receive His laws not as a heavy burden but as a delight and as a friend. They take us by the hand and lead us in the way of life, showing us how we can glorify and enjoy God forever. The Ten Commandments are a rule of life because they reflect the moral character of God.

TALKING POINTS

One of the key reasons Christians *seem* to be inconsistent is because those who are unfamiliar with the Bible may not understand how to properly read the Scriptures nor the importance of biblical *context*.

We are *His* people and He is *our* God, only because Jesus has become our great Covenant Keeper.

As those who are justified and adopted into God's family, we receive His laws not as a heavy burden but as a delight and as a friend.

DISCUSSION QUESTIONS

1. Why are the historical, literary, and redemptive contexts important for making appropriate applications of biblical teachings?

2. What is a covenant, and how can you see the unity of Scripture through the various covenants of the Bible?

3. What is the moral law of God, and why does it have an ongoing binding character, unlike the various dietary and ceremonial laws we find in the first five books of the Bible?

PART TWO

THE ART OF CENSORSHIP

6

MAKING GOD IN OUR IMAGE

Censoring Scripture is an art. And as with most things, it takes a blend of natural ability and practice, nature and nurture.

Unfortunately, the American church has become good at cherry-picking from the Scriptures those warm and fuzzy verses that make us feel good. We seem afraid of what people might think if we call certain behaviors a sin or affirm "difficult" doctrines such as the sovereignty and justice of God, His creation of all things, or the reality of hell, to name a few.

The art of censoring is also the name of the church-growth game. We believe (albeit falsely) that if we preach and teach only those feel-good verses to young soul-patch hipsters week by week (or "lumbersexuals," as the case may be), then the church will grow. And who can complain about a growing church?

But here's the problem: We confuse church growth with church health. We think a church is healthy if it has an in-house Starbucks, bookstore, escalators, and media center and thousands flocking through the doors each Sunday. While many growing churches are also healthy, we shouldn't equate the two. From T-shirts to church camps, from seminary lectures to sermons, Christ's sheep are routinely fed an unbalanced diet. And digesting only half the counsel of God's Word doesn't provide the spiritual nutrients needed for healthy, faithful, and biblical growth. We're big in the head and small in the body.

In the pages that follow, I want to explore the art of censoring the Scriptures by looking at seven of the most commonly censored topics in the Bible. I also want to show you why you can confidently embrace these topics and give you some practical ways—some guardrails—to maintain both faith and humility at the same time.

THE HALF-COUNSEL OF GOD

We are made in the image of God (Gen. 1:27), not the other way around. He is the Creator and we are the creation. He is the Potter and we are the clay. By His grace, He molds and forms us into the likeness and holiness of His Son. The American church desperately needs to reclaim a *God*-centered faith—one that begins with the freedom and glory of God, not the freedom and glory of man.

It seems as though many self-professing Christians prefer a tame, cuddly, grandpa-like god to the actual God revealed in the pages of Scripture. We're embarrassed when we read that God "shall strike the earth with the rod of his mouth, and with the breath of his lips he shall kill the wicked" (Isa. 11:4). Then—like a televised version of an R-rated movie—we bleep out the bad parts, "creating" a new god in the process.

Of course, we don't intentionally aim to censor the Scriptures, but we functionally do this without realizing it. We functionally proclaim the *half*-counsel of God. And it is precisely the *character of God* that some find very disturbing. But we don't need to be disturbed or embarrassed by God.

A GOD-CENTERED LIFE

Jonathan Edwards (1703–1758), the early American theologian and revivalist preacher of the First Great Awakening, captured well this God-centeredness of the Christian life. He had what some have called a "God entranced vision of all things."[1] Edwards argued that God's goal, His mission, is to be glorified above all else. The praise and worship of God is the purpose for which He created the world.

You might object at this point: "Well, if that's true, then God is just a self-centered egomaniac." But if God were to pursue any goal *other* than His own glory, it would be idolatry. Think about it. He would be elevating the creation above Himself, the Creator. It is necessary and right that God's chief end is to glorify Himself, *for our sake*. Here's what Edwards wrote:

> Because [God] infinitely values his own glory, consisting in the knowledge of himself, love to himself and complacence and joy in himself; he therefore valued the image, communication, or participation of these in the creature. And it is because he values himself, that he delights in the knowledge, and

love, and joy of the creature; as being himself the object of this knowledge, love, and complacence.[2]

To *glorify* God is to treasure Him, praise Him, trust Him, love Him, and to value what He values (namely, Himself) above all else.

Our chief end—as the Westminster divines famously expressed (1640s)—is "to glorify God and to enjoy him forever."[3] And the primary way in which we glorify God is to enjoy and treasure Him above all else. As John Piper has oftentimes said, "God is most glorified in us when we are most satisfied in him." Notice how utterly *God*-centered this perspective is. Paul wrote, "For from him and through him and to him are all things. To him be glory forever" (Rom. 11:36). That all things exist for God's glory and praise gives us a refreshing respite in a world of self-help and self-empowerment.

We desperately need to reclaim the centrality, power, authority, glory, majesty, wonder, holiness, and sovereign grace of God in our preaching, teaching, and worship. We need to reclaim His wisdom and His design for our families and churches, our vocations, parenting, and ministries of mercy to the poor and the outcast. Our theology and faith need to be dripping with a humble joy in the greatness of God.

PURSUING PASSION WITHOUT KNOWLEDGE

Growing up, I had what you might call a "little-man" complex. My friends labeled me "Small Fry" at an early age, and I made it my mission to prove them wrong. While I loved soccer and running—which came naturally to me—I *wanted* to play baseball. But because

I lacked the natural faculty to stay calm and stationary, my dad (rightly) insisted that I get my energy out running after a soccer ball rather than standing in the outfield and waiting for a ball to come my way. Thus, my high school baseball career found an outlet only in PE class.

During PE, the students converged on the diamond to choose teams, which I hated. Yes, I was that nervous last pick, impatiently waiting for the makeshift draft to end. When I stepped up to the plate, however, I wanted to overcome my little-man complex, and so I would swing with all my might. I believed in swinging for the fence—go big or go home—but I always struck out.

Many Christians today believe in swinging for the fence. They want to be passionate, "sold-out," radical followers of Jesus, but they're giving it their all for the wrong god. Just because some people are passionate doesn't mean their lifestyles are healthy or right. You can be passionate about all sorts of unhealthy, harmful things, such as mullets, porn, or the mysterious McRib sandwich. When we invent a god in our image—like a divine buddy who is at times weak, pouty, and needy—we are no longer talking about the God of the Bible.

The apostle Paul wanted to see his fellow Jews come to saving faith in Christ. But he was distraught that so many had rejected the gospel. He wrote to the Roman Christians, "Brothers, my heart's desire and prayer to God for them is that they may be saved. For I bear them witness that they have a zeal for God, *but not according to knowledge*" (Rom. 10:1–2).

You can have zeal and passion, but if it is not according to the truth of Scripture, you remain lost. This doesn't mean that you can know God fully or completely, but it does mean that you can know

Him truly. Having a right knowledge of God is key. As Hosea said, "My people are destroyed for lack of knowledge" (Hos. 4:6). But because we sometimes feel uncomfortable (unnecessarily) by our lack of understanding of the true and living God of Scripture, we end up censoring some of His attributes.

JESUS DOWN THE CHIMNEY

In December of 2003, I took a temporary job as Santa Claus for the Sprint phone company in Chattanooga, Tennessee. Because I was an awkward, shy college student, they were scraping the bottom of the barrel. I'm not sure if Santa has pimples, but he certainly did that December.

Every day, the Frosty the Snowman air blew through streets between the tall office buildings downtown, and I stood at a busy intersection and waved to the passing cars and pedestrians. Every now and then, I would bellow, "Ho, ho, ho! Merry Christmas!"

I quickly learned that people hated Santa. I've never been cussed out or flipped the bird more times in my life. One particular young man let such a steady stream of filth flow from his mouth that I wanted to extend the right fist of fellowship. But I didn't want to see the newspaper headline "Santa Decks Kid" the next day, so I just smiled and waved.

If you listen closely to the songs and stories of Christmas, you might begin to wonder about the powers of Old St. Nick. Think about it. He sees you at all times, whether you're sleeping or awake. He even knows your behavior, whether you've been good or bad. Sounds awfully similar to the omniscience of God.

"Oh, c'mon!" you might say. "Is it really so bad?" Maybe it is. Whenever people exchange the glory of God for a man-made myth—*and then teach it to millions of children as fact*—we despise His character and demote Him to a divine grandpa who gives us toys when we've been good, as if we've earned them. What's more, we begin to develop a subconscious correlation between the attributes of Santa and the attributes of God.

The difference between coming down a chimney and being born in a manger might not seem that great, but if you ask most self-professing Christians how to be saved, you could easily replace "God" with "Santa" in their descriptions. He's the rewarder of good behavior. All you have to do is be nice and loving and you'll get a ride on the one-horse open sleigh to glory. And there, in that wonderland of glory, we'll always be together. But, of course, only if the fates allow.

From the White House to Hollywood, Americans are constantly imbibing a watered-down, lifeless, impotent god. We see this god on the big screen, hear about him on the local country radio station, and invoke his presence during times of national tragedy. But is this the triune and sovereign God of the universe? Are we good simply because we use the word *god*, or do our words lack true meaning? Make no mistake: there is no actual generic god, made in our image, but only the true and living God as revealed in Scripture.

REAFFIRMING GOD AS TRINITY

One way we can reaffirm the God of Scripture is to reaffirm God *as* Trinity—Father, Son, and Holy Spirit—one God in three persons. He is not three gods (tritheism), nor is He one God with three masks (modalism). The Father is God, but He's not the Son. The Son is God, but He's not the Spirit. The Spirit is God, but He's not the Father or the Son. The three persons of the Godhead are equal in power, glory, eternity, and majesty.

I love robust Trinitarian worship, something I'm continuing to study and experience. Unfortunately, it's missing in many evangelical churches today. I remember preaching a sermon from Romans 7 for a seminary class. I carefully explained the exegetical nuances of the Greek, placed the text in its historical and redemptive contexts, and made appropriate application. Or so I thought. But when my fellow classmates gave me feedback, one man asked, "Where is the Holy Spirit?" I realized that I rarely ever think about, talk about, or incorporate a truly Trinitarian perspective in my life because I somehow affirm the Father, Son, and Holy Bible, but leave out the Spirit. I have a lot to learn.

According to a 2014 LifeWay Research poll, 58 percent of those who classify themselves as "evangelical" affirm that the Holy Spirit is a force, *not* a personal being.[4] In other words, even among the most conservative branch of American "Christianity," less than half affirm the personhood of the Spirit. This is the same Spirit who is grieved (Eph. 4:30), who teaches (John 14:26), who convicts (John 16:8), who inspires (2 Pet. 1:21), who is lied to (Acts 5:3–4), and who is sinned against (Matt. 12:32). We *all* have a lot to learn.

REAFFIRMING THE ATTRIBUTES OF GOD

Part of our functional embarrassment over "offensive" passages in Scripture stems from a low view of God. I'll explain this a bit later, but we can't imagine that God would kill people or, much less, send people to hell. Our theology tends to promote humanity and demote God. We tend to think of ourselves as generally good and are confused when bad things happen to good people.[5]

When Christians pray, they sometimes use the acronym ACTS, which stands for adoration, confession, thanksgiving, and supplication. It's a helpful guide to orient your heart and mind in prayer. When I examine my own prayer life, I usually emphasize the reverse: STCA. It seems that 90 percent of my prayers are asking God for things. Yes, I will *thank* Him and sometimes *confess* my sin. But how often do I simply *adore* Him and praise Him for who He is?

Scripture reveals a number of attributes and characteristics of God. All of these attributes should shift our thinking so that we are transformed by the renewing of our minds according to the truth of Scripture (Rom. 12:2). In my opinion, here are ten of the most prominent and often-overlooked attributes of God we find in the Bible:[6]

1. *God is sovereign.* He is in complete control over all things. Not the fiercest tornado, tiniest molecule, or falling sparrow is outside the control, power, and will of God (Job 37:9; Matt. 10:29). He does all that pleases Him, and He is never surprised, confused, or lacking absolute power. He decrees all that happens and brings those events about in time and space. This does not mean that we are mere robots. To be sure, we are responsible beings. But in

God's control and power over His creation, He
declares "the end from the beginning and from
ancient times things not yet done" (Isa. 46:10).
God "works all things according to the counsel
of his will" (Eph. 1:11). Proverbs teaches, "The
lot is cast into the lap, but its every decision
is from the LORD" (16:33). Even the death of
Christ was "according to the definite plan and
foreknowledge of God" (Acts 2:23). The reason
you can trust God's promises in the Bible is
precisely because He is sovereign to fulfill those
promises. The reason why you pray is because
you believe God can "do far more abundantly
than all that we ask or think" (Eph. 3:20).

2. *God is holy.* Even though we are created in the
   image of God, He is wholly set apart as the
   Creator. Unlike us, He is altogether unique,
   perfect, and righteous. "To whom then will
   you compare me, that I should be like him?
   says the Holy One" (Isa. 40:25). God's holiness
   conveys two primary meanings: (1) God is
   utterly set apart and distinct from His creation,
   and (2) He is morally perfect. In Him there is
   no moral darkness at all (1 John 1:5). He is
   completely pure in thought, word, and deed.
   He is supremely good. We can "enter his gates
   with thanksgiving, and his courts with praise."
   Why? "For the LORD is good" (Ps. 100:4–5).

Christians are called holy only because God
declares us holy.[7] But we are not intrinsically
and inherently holy. God, on the other hand,
is "holy, holy, holy" (Isa. 6:3) in His being and
character. And one day, the heavenly throng
will exult together, saying, "For you alone are
holy" (Rev. 15:4).

3. *God is wise.* I'm good at giving God advice on
how to run His universe, or at least I think I am.
But who can really give God advice or counsel?
As the apostle Paul proclaimed, "Oh, the depth
of the riches and wisdom and knowledge of
God! How unsearchable are his judgments and
how inscrutable his ways! 'For who has known
the mind of the Lord, or who has been his
counselor?'" (Rom. 11:33–34). God's wisdom
is *right knowledge expressed rightly.* Thus, it
has a moral component to it. His wisdom is
like Joseph's coat of many colors—a myriad
of threads woven together into a beautiful
tapestry of His delight—"so that through the
church the manifold wisdom of God might
now be made known ... according to [His]
eternal purpose" (Eph. 3:10–11).

4. *God is love.* This is a favorite among evangelicals,
and for good reason! Without God's love, He
would not have sent His only begotten Son
(John 3:16). The apostle John taught, "God is

love, and whoever abides in love abides in God, and God abides in him" (1 John 4:16). From all eternity, God the Father, God the Son, and God the Holy Spirit are held in the unity of love (see John 17:20–24). God demonstrates His benevolent love through the giving of His Son: "God shows his love for us in that while we were still sinners, Christ died for us" (Rom. 5:8). And God's love for us is free and unconditional with regard to our love for Him. In fact, we love only because He first loved us (1 John 4:19). God loves us because of the finished work of His Son on the cross—and not our behavior— therefore, nothing in all of creation will be able "to separate us from the love of God in Christ Jesus our Lord" (Rom. 8:39). John Piper, summarizing Jonathan Edwards, wrote about God's love: "The love of God for sinners is not his making much of them, but his graciously freeing and empowering them to enjoy making much of him."[8] The reason He loves you is chiefly for His own glory.

5. *God is gracious.* Due to the endless stream of advertisements on TV, radio, and the Internet, we can easily start thinking that we *deserve* an endless amount of stuff. We believe that we are *entitled* to health, wealth, and prosperity—that it is our *right* to have these things. But God

alone has all rights. He has no obligation to show you grace or mercy. If so, it wouldn't be called grace or mercy! Both the Old Testament and the New Testament affirm this: "I will be gracious to whom I will be gracious, and will show mercy on whom I will show mercy" (Exod. 33:19; cf. Rom. 9:15). Paul added, "So then it depends not on human will or exertion, but on God, who has mercy" (Rom. 9:16). We deserve the wages of our sin: death. "But God"—the two greatest words in the Bible—"made us alive together with Christ—by grace you have been saved" (Eph. 2:4–6).

6. *God is just.* Unlike God's love and grace, which evangelicals are quick to plaster on bumper stickers and Twitter, God's justice is rarely mentioned. Ask yourself: When is the last time you've been particularly thankful that God is just? God's justice can be understood in two interrelated ways. First, He is the equitable ruler of all. He executes justice for the oppressed and the abused. Second, God punishes sin and rights the wrongs. Because God is just, He will not let the child molester off the hook. He will not turn a blind eye to genocide. Nor will He let your sin slide by. If you're a Christian, God has satisfied His own justice by punishing your sin on the cross of Christ. In this way, He

is both "just and the justifier of the one who has faith in Jesus" (Rom. 3:26). Christian, you have no more hell to pay.

7. *God is unchanging.* Also referred to as God's immutability, this means that He remains "the same yesterday and today and forever" (Heb. 13:8). He has "no variation or shadow due to change" (James 1:17). The psalmist declared that even though the heavens and the earth will pass away, "you are the same, and your years have no end" (Ps. 102:27). God's being, attributes, and will do not change. He cannot be improved or grow into something greater than He already is. God doesn't suddenly lose His knowledge or sovereignty. He doesn't change into an unjust mongrel or divine tyrant. Because He doesn't change, we can "trust in the LORD forever, for the LORD GOD is an everlasting rock" (Isa. 26:4). Because God's sovereign love doesn't change, He will never let go of His bride, the church. When Scripture speaks of God "changing" His mind, it speaks only as it *seems* from our perspective. But God does not change or progress. R. C. Sproul explained, "When our understanding of God changes, it is not because God has changed. We are the ones who change. God doesn't grow. God doesn't improve with age. God is the Lord everlasting."[9]

8. *God is everywhere.* Also called God's omnipresence, His capacity to be everywhere means *not* that He becomes one with the rocks and trees. That would be closer to pantheism. Rather, it means that, because God is eternal Spirit (John 4:24), His divine presence is throughout the universe. He dwells in His creation but remains distinct from it as the Creator. Moreover, He does not exist more in some places and less in others. He is everywhere, fully present. King David prayed, "Where shall I go from your Spirit? Or where shall I flee from your presence?" (Ps. 139:7). We cannot escape the presence of God. As God told Jeremiah, "Am I a God at hand, declares the LORD, and not a God far away? Can a man hide himself in secret places so that I cannot see him? declares the LORD. Do I not fill heaven and earth? declares the LORD" (Jer. 23:23–24). Because of this, believers can treasure the reality that He is *Immanuel*—"God with us"—in the person of Jesus Christ, who "became flesh and dwelt among us" (John 1:14).

9. *God is all-knowing.* God knows everything. He knows everything about the origins of the universe, everything about calculus, everything about chemistry, and everything about you. He knows the number of hairs (or lack thereof!) on your head (Luke 12:7). We would do well

to echo the psalmist: "O LORD, you have searched me and known me! You know when I sit down and when I rise up; you discern my thoughts from afar ... Even before a word is on my tongue, behold, O LORD, you know it altogether" (Ps. 139:1–4). Jesus was fully God and fully man. In His *humanity*, He increased in wisdom (Luke 2:52). But His divine nature never lacked knowledge. God knows every thought, word, and deed. He knew that you would be reading this page right now. He knew that Adam and Eve would fall into sin (Gen. 3), that David would commit adultery with Bathsheba (2 Sam. 11), and that He would send His Son to die for sinners (Acts 2:23). In God's eternal foreknowledge, the Lamb was slain, as it were, from before the foundation of the world (Rev. 13:8).

10. *God is self-sufficient.* That God is self-sufficient means that He is complete in Himself from all eternity. He does not need you or me. He is dependent on nothing and no one. Even in our worship, we do not give God something that He doesn't already possess. He didn't create the world just because He was lonely and needed a friend. No, He created the world for the continued praise of His own name. But even if the church crumbled and the world went to hell in a

handbasket, He would still make a great name for Himself. He is self-existent and uncreated. He's not lacking in any way, but complete and perfect in His being. This attribute of God alone should cause us to pause in humility and consider His greatness and majesty.

THE CHARACTER OF GOD AND DIFFICULT VERSES

God said, "Be still, and know that I am God" (Ps. 46:10). If we stopped and anchored our knowledge in God as He is revealed in Scripture—acknowledging the various attributes listed above—we would have a better perspective on the many difficult and "offensive" texts we find in the Bible. Let me give you two related examples, one from a well-known story and the other from the Psalms.

First, in Genesis 6–8, we read about the worldwide flood during the days of Noah. When we think of the story of Noah and the flood, we typically think of cute animals painted on the walls of Sunday school nurseries, with Noah and all his furry friends looking out the windows of the ark, smiling. It's interesting what *isn't* shown or talked about. Why? We're embarrassed about the reality of God's justice and wrath against sin. Rather than talking about the reason for the flood, we talk about the animals—two by two, one pink and one blue—and wonder how Noah packed them all in there.

However, the story of Noah and the ark isn't just about zebras and turtles; it's about God's justice and mercy. It's about His justice against sin and His mercy toward Noah and his family. Was it wrong for God to wipe out humanity from the face of the earth? Can we bring legitimate charges of injustice against Him? Genesis 6:5 says, "The LORD saw that the wickedness of man was great in the earth, and that every intention of the thoughts of his heart was only evil continually." The wages of sin are death, and sinful humanity earned their payment in full.

But let me drive this closer to home with a question: Should we *praise* God for killing wicked humanity? Yes, sort of. We don't rejoice sadistically because people die. Even God doesn't take pleasure in the death of the wicked (Ezek. 18:23). But we *do* praise God because He is glorified in the display of justice. He has given an appropriate and right punishment for their wickedness.

Praise will be Christians' response when God judges the unbelieving world at the end of the age. From the book of Revelation, we read that Christian martyrs will plead with Him, "O Sovereign Lord, holy and true, how long before you will judge and avenge our blood on those who dwell on the earth?" (6:10). The unbelieving world—symbolized by "Babylon"—rejects God and His Word. As for His people, God tells them, "Rejoice over [Babylon], O heaven, and you saints and apostles and prophets, for God has given judgment for you against her" (18:20). Rejoice? Yes, because God settles accounts and makes the wrongs right.

Second, consider the "imprecatory psalms"—those prayers and petitions that call down God's judgment on unbelieving, sinful humanity. Two of the most notorious are Psalms 58 and 59. Here are some of the verses we find there:

- "O God, break the teeth in their mouths" (58:6).

- "Let them be like the snail that dissolves into slime, like the stillborn child who never sees the sun" (58:8).
- "Rouse yourself to punish all the nations; spare none of those who treacherously plot evil" (59:5).
- "For the cursing and lies that they utter, consume them in wrath; consume them till they are no more" (59:12–13).

Would you pray any of these verses? How do *these* fit with "Jesus Loves Me"? These verses would make most Christians today blush and squirm with embarrassment. If we were leading a Bible study on the Psalms, we might be tempted to conveniently skip over these passages and cling to the last verse of Psalm 59: "O my Strength, I will sing praises to you, for you O God, are my fortress, the God who shows me steadfast love" (v. 17).

But do we really need to be embarrassed? Is it wrong for God to punish sin? Of course not; He's just and holy. Remember that (if you're a believer) your sin has *already* been punished on the cross. Jesus drank the bitter cup of suffering for you. If there is any sense of injustice in our bones, we should be rattled to the core when we look to the suffering of Jesus. The only righteous One who ever walked this earth was nailed to a cross of wood for sin He didn't commit. Why? Paul answered: "For our sake he made him to be sin who knew no sin, so that in him we might become the righteousness of God" (2 Cor. 5:21).

May we unashamedly praise God for His character and attributes. Scripture doesn't contradict itself. The death of Noah's contemporaries and David's enemies glorified God, not because He takes delight in the death of the wicked, but because He has executed justice for sin. May we desire to be shaped and molded and made into God's image, not Him into our image.

TALKING POINTS

It seems as though many self-professing Christians prefer a tame, cuddly, grandpa-like god to the actual God revealed in the pages of Scripture.

Our theology and faith need to be dripping with a humble joy in the greatness of God.

Many Christians today believe in swinging for the fence. They want to be passionate, "sold-out," radical followers of Jesus, but they're giving it their all for the wrong god.

DISCUSSION QUESTIONS

1. Have you noticed a de-emphasis on the person and work of the Holy Spirit in contemporary Christian theology and worship?

2. What are some of the more "difficult" attributes of God for you to talk about and enjoy?

3. Read through Psalm 59. How does this chapter give glory to God? How might it point us to the need and work of Jesus Christ?

7

COVERING UP CREATION

In the fall of 2014, Peter Enns, professor of biblical studies at Eastern University, released a book titled *The Bible Tells Me So: Why Defending Scripture Has Made Us Unable to Read It.*[1] Enns was let go from Westminster Theological Seminary in 2008 over his unorthodox views of Scripture. With the release of his book, I can see that not much has changed.

In *The Bible Tells Me So*, Enns's purpose is to "liberate" anxiety-ridden conservative Christians from the pressure of having to protect the Bible from threats made against it. Enns argues that we should embrace the "messiness" of the Bible—its errors, contradictions, and all. The publisher tells us the intended impact: "In *The Bible Tells Me So*, Enns wants to do for the Bible what Rob Bell did for hell in *Love Wins*."[2] While Bell "freed" people from the historic belief in hell, Enns wants to "free" people from the historic belief in the Bible. Problem solved.

The book reads like William Wallace heroically freeing naive evangelicals from the shackles of conservative doctrine. Enns might even paint his face blue. But is this a fair judgment of conservative Christianity? Are we in need of "liberating" from an old-fashioned faith?

IS GENESIS A FAIRY TALE?

Enns has written a considerable amount on creation and the Genesis account. In *The Bible Tells Me So*, he argued, "You don't have to go beyond the first two books of the Bible, Genesis and Exodus, to find stories that are hard to take at face value and read more like scripts for a fairy tale."[3] He went on to describe the rather fictitious nature (as he sees it) of creation, the story of Adam and Eve, the serpent in the garden, and the other miraculous events of Genesis. Ironically, Enns pointed out exactly what I've been arguing in this book:

> There's a reason pastors' sermons and Bible study
> groups don't spend a lot of time in these sections:
> it's hard to know what to do with all this, and there
> doesn't seem to be a lot of payoff in investing the
> effort to try. Other parts of the Bible are shocking
> to read, even barbaric, and hard to defend as the
> Word of God in civil adult conversation.[4]

I agree. But we arrive at two very different conclusions. While Enns would have you take a patronizing seat high above the "fairy-tale" Bible stories of creation, the fall, the flood, and the Red Sea, I would affirm these events as described in the biblical text. I would embrace them by a reasonable faith, as I do Christ's atonement for my sin (now *that's* miraculous!). And I would also ask: What did Jesus and the New Testament authors think about these events? Did they think they were fairy tales or historical realities?

RUNNING FROM CREATION

Enns isn't alone in this post-evangelical world. Self-professing Christians of all stripes seem to be running from the creation account in Genesis like those loonies running from the bulls in Pamplona. Or maybe they're just running from their prehistoric ancestors. In any case, Christians don't know how to reconcile Genesis with what we've been taught by our government and the natural history museums. I mean, our government education and natural history museums can't be biased, right?

But why would they be running? The answer is simple: because they're embarrassed by the Bible. They cherry-pick those texts that can be "scientifically" verified and censor the rest to freeze along with the Ice Age. The issue of creation is like the off-the-rocker uncle at Thanksgiving or the locked-up chaos in your closet when company comes over. Just don't let people know about it. God's creation account is barely whispered from the pulpit and eliminated from the radio. Besides, football is much more interesting.

Here is what's happening: Evangelicals are running to "science" *first* and *then* attempting to make the creation account fit within that "science." We'll look at some examples of science later, but it's important to see the order. Why do Christians do this? We don't do this for any other doctrine. You don't go down to the morgue and wait for somebody to rise from the dead in order to believe in the resurrection. You don't try walking on water in the Okefenokee Swamp in order to believe that Jesus walked to His disciples in such a manner. Why do we do this with *creation*? It's because we believe that the all-knowing Darwin has spoken and that the unbiased natural history museums and *National Geographic* have proved his theory once for all.

WHAT DOES GENESIS ACTUALLY TEACH?

When you study the creation account in Genesis 1 and 2, you find God creating all things out of nothing in the span of six days:

- Day 1: formless planet, light, rotating earth
- Day 2: earth's atmosphere, separation of atmospheric and oceanic waters
- Day 3: dry land, vegetation, plants, fruit trees
- Day 4: sun, moon, stars
- Day 5: water creatures and birds
- Day 6: land animals, Adam and Eve

Immediately, your red flag might go up in regard to light being created on day 1 and the sun being created on day 4. How can you have light without the sun? This has led some Christians to see this as poetry (the framework hypothesis), linking the days in two columns:

Day 1—Day 4
Day 2—Day 5
Day 3—Day 6

They *sort of* go together. But forcing this paradigm on the text is unnecessary and does not fully consider the historical, literary, and redemptive contexts, as we shall see in a moment.

If we cringe at believing in the existence of light *apart* from the sun, then we will also run into problems when God's glory will give light in the new heavens and the new earth. In Revelation, we see that the New Jerusalem "has no need of sun or moon to shine on it, for the glory of God gives it light" (Rev. 21:23). The apostle John added, "They will need no light of lamp or sun, for the Lord God will be their light" (22:5).

Linking Genesis to Revelation on this point is appropriate. There are some striking parallels between Genesis and these last chapters of Revelation: the mention of the "tree of life" (Gen. 2:9; Rev. 22:2, 14, 19), the new "heaven" and new "earth" (Gen. 1:1; Rev. 21:1), and the reversal of pain and death (Gen. 3:16–19; Rev. 21:4), to name a few. Shouldn't we let Scripture interpret Scripture? Is it really so hard to believe that God would be the source of light (day 1) before transferring that light to His created luminaries (day 4)? At heart, we don't want to look foolish in the eyes of the world. We're willing to be "fools for Christ's sake" (1 Cor. 4:10), but not over the issue of creation.

LITERARY GENRE

It is beyond the scope and purpose of this chapter to give a detailed analysis of the creation account and the many theories surrounding it. This has been done elsewhere.[5] However, I want to summarize some of the salient reasons for taking Genesis 1 and 2 as they plainly read. First, we need to comprehend the meaning of the text as the author intended. To do this, we need to understand its genre—the type of literature it is. So we ask: Is Genesis 1 a letter? Is it poetry? Is it a proverb for ethical living?

I believe that the literary genre of Genesis 1 is *historical narrative*. One of the strongest reasons for this is what's called the consecutive *waw* (pronounced "vawv"), which appears throughout the Hebrew text. The consecutive *waw* is a single Hebrew letter attached as a prefix to a verb and translated simply as our English "and." Go to Genesis 1 and begin reading. You will notice the word "and" over and over and over again: "*And* God said, 'Let there be light,' *and* there was light. *And* God saw that the light was good. *And* God separated the light from the darkness" (Gen. 1:3–4). You get the idea. The consecutive *waw* shows up in historical narrative passages of the Old Testament (such as the Samuels, Kings, Chronicles, and so on) because it is the earmark of historical narrative. In other words, Genesis 1 should be read *as history*, not as poetry or epistle. Most evangelicals don't question the historical accounts of these other Old Testament books, so why do we question the record of creation? The primary reason is that we want to somehow make Genesis 1 "fit" Darwinian evolution.

Another reason to take Genesis 1 and 2 as historical narratives is because of the number of finite verbs (those that carry the action, rather than imperatives or cohortatives) as equivalent to other sections of historical narrative in the Old Testament.[6] Third, the simple and plain reading of Genesis 1 is a historical account of what took place during the creation week. Fourth, Jesus and the New Testament writers understood the historical-literal nature of Genesis when they quoted from it.[7] Fifth, biblical scholar Walter Kaiser noted that

Genesis 1–11 contains sixty-four geographical names, eighty-eight personal names, forty-eight generic names, and twenty-one identifiable cultural items.[8] Add to this the fact that Genesis 10 itself has five times more geographical data than that of the entire Koran! Genesis 1–11 was not written as myth, poetry, or prophecy, but as *history*.

THE LENGTH OF "DAYS"

It is popular to read "day" as long periods of time to fit the perceived age of the earth (day-age theory, analogical, and so forth). We'll get to some of this in a moment. But for now we need to note that the normal, straightforward reading of the "days" in Genesis 1—*yom* in Hebrew—is the twenty-four-hour day. Yes, *yom* can mean longer periods of time *when necessitated by the genre or the context*.[9] The genre, as noted earlier, is historical narrative. So as to remove all doubt, the writer added the recurring "evening and morning." Outside of Genesis 1, in every instance where *yom* is used with either "evening" or "morning" (twenty-three times), it is always a literal twenty-four-hour day. The days are also qualified by numbers (first, second, and so on), signaling literal twenty-four-hour days.

Significantly, in the establishment of the Ten Commandments, Exodus 20:11 states, "For in six days the LORD made heaven and earth, the sea, and all that is in them, and rested on the seventh day" (see also Exod. 31:17). Do you see the correlation? The creation week was used to establish the Sabbath day. Or, to put it the other way around, the foundation of the fourth commandment is the literal six-day creation week. It would not make sense any other way. Genesis 2 is simply a more detailed description of the events of day six.

Jesus believed that the first man, Adam, was created *not* after millions or billions of years but from the very beginning. When speaking to the Pharisees on marriage and divorce, He told them, "Have you not read that he who created them *from the beginning* made them male and female" (Matt. 19:4; see also Mark 10:6). How could there be billions of years before Adam and Eve when they were created "from the beginning"? Jesus's own knowledge and interpretation of the creation record understood it to be a normal week, with Adam and Eve being created on the sixth day.

THEOLOGICAL SIGNIFICANCE

With the fall in Genesis 3, death entered the created world. Thus, you cannot have millions (or billions) of years of animals or humans living *and dying* before the fall. If the "days" were long ages, you would have all sorts of animals, fish, and birds living and dying before the fall, a position that is incompatible with the curse of the fall—death.[10]

If Genesis 1–11 is not historically accurate (but rather assumed to be poetry or metaphor), then the foundation of biblical revelation and even the gospel itself is severely undermined. We are presented not only with a Creator God in these opening chapters of Genesis but also with the fall of humanity. Without the fall, humans need no Savior. Moreover, without the first Adam, there would be no second Adam (see Rom. 5:12–21; 1 Cor. 15:42–49). Yet, the New Testament writers affirmed the historical reality of Adam and Eve.

As we will briefly see below, the Noahic flood (Gen. 6–9) and Babel experience (Gen. 11) explain much of the scientific, geological, hydrodynamic, and anthropological realities that we see in the world today. Jesus Himself used the historical reality of the Noahic flood to describe the future reality of judgment: "Just as it was in the days of Noah, so will it be in the days of the Son of Man. They were eating and drinking and marrying and being given in marriage, until the day when Noah entered the ark, and the flood came and destroyed them all" (Luke 17:26–27). Both the writer of Hebrews (11:7) and the apostle Peter (1 Pet. 3:20) described Noah's flood as a historical event. Why do we question these events and censor them from our discussion?

IS CREATION AT ODDS WITH SCIENCE?

Several months ago, I walked into a bookstore with a name that rhymes with Hooks-A-Zillion. I was actually impressed with their selection of religious titles. I perused the theology and Bible sections and then noticed something rather ironic. Directly across the aisle from the biblical resources stood the science shelf. The two seemed to be staring each other down in a deadly duel, and I was caught in the middle!

To my admittedly limited understanding, the theory of evolution seems completely absurd. Think about it. For billions of years, rain falls on the rocks, making a sort of primordial goo. Then one day, the soup comes alive (without being killed by oxidation); it morphs and grows in complexity until—voilà!—living, breathing, reproducing human beings. And we think the creation narrative in Genesis is hard to believe? I would argue that it takes *lesser* faith to believe in creation than in evolution.

The simple fact is this: There has never been any kind of observable, testable, and repeatable evidence that evolution has ever taken place. While I affirm that mutations occur (microevolution) within their kinds, the theory of macroevolution has never been proved. Moreover, no evolutionist knows how we simply got life from non-life. The best explanation some can think of is that aliens brought life to earth millions of years ago. They cannot explain the problem of the Cambrian explosion or the complexity of early trilobites. Stephen Meyer's *New York Times* bestseller *Darwin's Doubt* should at least cause the modern skeptic to pause and consider the evidence against their firmly held presuppositions.[11]

In contrast to this, we should trust the only One who was actually there at the beginning, God Himself. Today, many notable scientists—with PhDs in geology, astronomy, and astrophysics from some of the world's leading universities—are rejecting evolutionary theory; and many of these are not Christians. If you are interested in some scholarly research in the area of creation science, I encourage you to explore the Institute for Creation Research (icr.org). But let me give you a few items to whet your appetite before we conclude.

First, Noah had plenty of room on his ark. He needed only two of each animal *according to its kind* (Gen. 7:14). For example, dogs, wolves, coyotes, foxes, and so on are all part of the same "kind." The genetic variations between these species were already present within the *kind*, "dog."

Second, the Noahic flood (Gen. 6–9) was a global, yearlong, catastrophic event that caused tremendous geological, atmospheric, hydrodynamic, and biological changes. Continents separated, mountains formed, and canyons were created. Lots of water over a short period of time, rather than a little water over a long period of time, explains much of the geological and fossil record we find today.

As I'm sure you know, a massive amount of water can cause very rapid devastation.

Third, the formation of millions of fossils, by definition, testifies to a catastrophic event, such as the Noahic flood. Dead animals or fish only decay over time (or they're eaten); they don't fossilize unless something catastrophic occurs and they are buried rapidly. In other words, only with a cataclysmic event is it even possible to have millions of dead things fossilized all over the earth. Indeed, because of the flood, we find millions of dead things buried in rock layers laid down by water all over the earth.[12] We've found upside-down fossilized trees jutting through multiple layers of sediment, fossilized shellfish high in the Himalayas, and whale bones in the middle of the African desert. Only the Noahic flood can account for all of these anomalies. We've also been able to identify red blood cells and soft tissue in dinosaur bones, which testifies to their "young age," not millions of years old.

Fourth, what about the dinosaurs? God made both land animals and humans on the sixth day. They lived side by side because, before the fall, animals (dinosaurs included) were vegetarians. They lived peaceably together. The claws and sharp teeth were used for cracking nuts, chewing bamboo, and so on, not eating meat. We see this today, for example, in pandas, fruit bats, and squirrels. Sharp teeth or sharp claws do not mean that they were carnivorous. Moreover, most dinosaurs, especially the babies, were quite small and could fit easily on the ark. Noah didn't need to get the biggest dinosaurs he could find into the ark, just a boy and a girl.

Fifth, the "problem" of distant starlight can be explained by (1) a change in the speed of light, which is not necessarily constant over time; (2) the change in the rate of time, as Albert Einstein showed how the rate of time is affected by gravity and motion; (3) a time-zone understanding of universal and local time so that light traveling toward the earth is similar to a plane traveling west that will arrive at the same local time—light could leave a distant star on day four and reach earth on day four, cosmic local time; or (4) our sovereign God simply using *supernatural* means to accomplish His purposes in creating distant stars.[13] This, of course, would not be the only supernatural event ordained by God.

Finally, and in more of a sociological context, evolution is inherently racist. During the blistering-hot summer of 1925 in the little town of Dayton, Tennessee, the world witnessed the clash of ideas at the Scopes "monkey" trial. John Scopes, a high school science teacher, taught evolution in the public school, which violated Tennessee's Butler Act. The American Civil Liberties Union (ACLU) decided to fund the evolutionary defense, led by the famous defense attorney Clarence Darrow, while the three-time US presidential nominee William Jennings Bryan represented the prosecution.

At the heart of the Scopes trial was the *Civic Biology* textbook written by George William Hunter (published in 1914) and used by Scopes, which affirmed the following:

> The Races of Man.—At the present time there exist
> upon the earth five races or varieties of man, each
> very different from the other in instincts, social
> customs, and, to an extent, in structure. These are
> the Ethiopian or negro type, originating in Africa;
> the Malay or brown race, from the islands of the

Pacific; the American Indian; the Mongolian or yellow race, including the natives of China, Japan, and the Eskimos; and finally, *the highest type of all, the Caucasians, represented by the civilized white* inhabitants of Europe and America.[14]

This racism isn't too dissimilar to the subtitle from Charles Darwin's 1859 (in)famous book, the full title being: *On the Origin of Species by Means of Natural Selection; or, The Preservation of Favoured Races in the Struggle for Life*. Evolution is, from its foundation, racist.

The Bible, on the other hand, teaches that there is only one race—the *human* race. While both Christians and non-Christians have certainly been at fault over this issue of racism in the past and present, Christians should affirm that all humans are made in the image of God (Gen. 1:27). And like the rest of Genesis 1, this affirmation is not just poetry. Jesus has "ransomed people for God from every tribe and language and people and nation" (Rev. 5:9).

We don't need to cover up creation. God created the world by His design and for His delight. "The heavens declare the glory of God, and the sky above proclaims his handiwork" (Ps. 19:1). Even if it seems that twenty-first-century secularists have shown the Bible to be out of step with "science," realize that those same secularists are constantly shifting their own conclusions. Rather than trying to codify these shifting conclusions to make them "fit" with the biblical record, we should first seek to understand what that biblical record actually says and, through it, seek to understand the world around us. May we uncensor the text, dare to embrace the entire Bible, and let its superior wisdom be our foundation for life and worldview.

TALKING POINTS

The issue of creation is like the off-the-rocker uncle at Thanksgiving or the locked-up chaos in your closet when company comes over. Just don't let people know about it.

Jesus believed that the first man, Adam, was created *not* after millions or billions of years but from the very beginning.

Directly across the bookstore aisle from the biblical resources stood the science shelf. The two seemed to be staring each other down in a deadly duel, and I was caught in the middle!

DISCUSSION QUESTIONS

1. Why have so many come to believe that the Bible and science are at odds with each other?

2. What's the relationship between the days of the creation week (Gen. 1–2) and the fourth commandment (Exod. 20)? Why do you think this is important?

3. Why is the historical reality of Adam (in Genesis) so important for a healthy biblical theology of salvation in Christ? If Adam and the fall (Gen. 3) are simply poetic in nature, what would that mean for the need of a Savior?

8

MASKING THE REALITY OF SIN

According to a 2014 LifeWay Research poll, 51 percent of self-identified evangelicals believe that "most people by nature are good." More than 75 percent of mainline Protestants and Roman Catholics agreed with the same statement. What does this tell us? If we are fundamentally good, then we can contribute to our salvation, which brings us to the next finding: 54 percent of evangelicals agree that "an individual must contribute his/her own effort for personal salvation."[1]

Are we fundamentally good? Do we reach down into the goodness of our hearts to make up the difference of Christ's *un*finished work on our behalf? Of course not. Then why do so many evangelicals believe this? Simply put, we are masking the reality and heinousness of sin.

We're embarrassed by what Scripture has to say about sin, and so we, like Peter Pan, choose to think happy thoughts—evidenced by the recent bestsellers *Become a Better You*, *Your Best Life Now*, and *It's*

Your Time. We are censoring the Scriptures for a feel-good faith. We pluck out promises of victory and blessing and neglect the *s* word. But you and I would not experience *any* blessing apart from the sheer mercy of God in forgiving our sin.

WHERE DID SIN COME FROM?

You and I sin because we are sinners. We don't suddenly become sinners once we reach the "age of accountability" (whatever that is) and then sin for the first time. No, we have inherited a sin nature from our parents, and their parents, and their parents, all the way back to our *first* parents, Adam and Eve. There, in the garden of Eden, they rebelled against their Creator by setting themselves up in His place. Because Adam was our representative, we fell with him in his first sin (Rom. 5:12–21). Ever since, we've had an innate propensity toward rebellion and sin (see Ps. 51:5).

My two-year-old son is an expert in physics, especially when it comes to yogurt. Not too long ago, he sat in his high chair, staring intently into his yogurt cup, and then he looked up at me and smiled. "Yes?" I asked, as I fixed my morning coffee. He very deliberately held the almost-full yogurt cup over the edge of his high chair, directly above the carpeted floor. He smiled again. In the most authoritative, fatherly voice I could muster, I said, "Garrett, do not drop your yogurt." He smiled again and demonstrated his physics experiment—watching the white slime explode all over the place like the Stay Puft Marshmallow Man in *Ghostbusters*. Even though he was only two, he knew what "do not drop" meant. I didn't teach him to drop the yogurt (I promise). His rebellion was built in.

OUR PRECONVERSION STATE

It didn't take long before Adam's rebellion turned the world into a sour, despondent, and evil place. By the time of Noah, "the LORD saw that the wickedness of man was great in the earth, and that every intention of the thoughts of his heart was only evil continually" (Gen. 6:5). Our outward sinful actions are simply the fruit on the tree. Before God transforms us, that tree is rotten down to the roots. Jeremiah described it like this: "The heart is deceitful above all things, and desperately sick; who can understand it?" (Jer. 17:9). In other words, we don't even understand the manipulative nature of our own hearts.

Just when we start thinking that we're a little sick with sin, the New Testament—yes, that place with all the love and grace—provides a fuller picture of our desperate plight. In Ephesians 2, Paul provided three ways in which we are separated from God by sin. But before I explain these, I realize that what you're about to read may be offensive for some readers. But there's a reason Jesus died. We wouldn't have nailed just a nice guy to a cross. He was offensive and He died *for sinners*, like me. So as you read this, I pray that you will have a humble and receiving mind and heart.

First, the apostle Paul wrote, "And you were dead in the trespasses and sins" (Eph. 2:1). You're not just a little ill; you're spiritually dead. Dead people don't need medicine; they need life. Sometimes, I will hear a preacher describe our condition like a sick man on his deathbed. The doctor comes in, puts a spoonful of healing gospel medicine near the sick man's mouth, but the man must make that 1 percent effort to sit up and take it. However, the image in Ephesians is radically different. The doctor has already come in and pronounced the man dead. There is no 1 percent effort. Christ must come in and give him new life. This is why we read that God has "caused us to be born again" (1 Pet. 1:3). Jesus told Nicodemus—Nick at Nite—"you must be born again" by the Spirit of God (John 3:5–8).

Second, Paul said that we were *following* Satan, the "prince of the power of the air" (Eph. 2:2). Satan, the great deceiver, is not yet bound. He is creating havoc and doing what he is permitted to do against the kingdom of God. But we were Satan's servants because the "god of this world has blinded the minds of the unbelievers" (2 Cor. 4:4). After we were freed to love God because He first loved us, we became followers of Jesus. The founder of the Methodist Church, Charles Wesley (1707–1788), wrote in the hymn "And Can It Be That I Should Gain":

> 'Tis mercy all, immense and free;
> For O my God, it found out me....
> My chains fell off, my heart was free;
> I rose, went forth, and followed thee.

On the one-year anniversary of Wesley's conversion, he wrote "O for a Thousand Tongues to Sing," in which we find these words:

> O for a thousand tongues to sing
> My great Redeemer's praise;
> The glories of my God and King,
> The triumphs of his grace!

The grace of God broke our enslavement to sin and our service to Satan. Oh, that we would have a thousand tongues to sing God's praise!

Third, Paul taught that we were "children of wrath" (Eph. 2:3). Do you want to know something absolutely shocking? Not everybody in the world is a child of God. I know, that's offensive. But according to Scripture, while all humans are created in God's image, only Christians are His *children*. Through faith in Christ, we become His adopted children. Jesus alone is the eternal Son of God; we are brought into the family by law and by love. But before we became children of God through faith alone in Christ alone and by His grace alone, we were children of wrath.

As children of wrath, we were bent on following our own path of destruction. We did not seek God; He sought us. "None is righteous, no, not one; no one understands; no one seeks for God. All have turned aside; together they have become worthless; no one does good, not even one" (Rom. 3:10–12).

While we're at it, let me add one more possibly offensive thought here: Those who remain in their unbelief—apart from a saving relationship with God in Christ—*cannot* please God. In Romans 8, Paul contrasted the believer and the unbeliever. The believer's mind is set on the things of the Spirit while the unbeliever's mind is set on the things of sinful flesh. He wrote, "For the mind that is set on the flesh is hostile to God, for it does not submit to God's law; indeed, it cannot. *Those who are in the flesh cannot please God*" (vv. 7–8). The writer of Hebrews concurred: "Without faith it is impossible to please him" (11:6). These are not my words. All Scripture is breathed out by God; these are His words.

What does this mean? This means that even the unbelieving man handing out food in Haiti is not pleasing God. Why? Because he is not doing it for God, because of God, or in any way in service to God. He "cannot please God" apart from his union and relationship with Christ. The reason this might seem so offensive to our modern ears is because our theology is very man centered. As Martin Luther once wrote to his debate partner, Erasmus, "Your thoughts on God are far too human."[2]

WHEN CHRISTIANS SIN

Does sin suddenly disappear from our lives when we become Christians? If you think it has in your life, then you will need to consider what the apostle John wrote: "If we say we have no sin, we deceive ourselves, and the truth is not in us" (1 John 1:8). While the *presence* of sin hasn't disappeared from our lives, the *power* and *penalty* of sin have been vanquished. It no longer dominates and enslaves our souls. The wages of sin—the penalty of death and hell—have been "paid in full" by our Lord. "Paid in full" is the literal Greek meaning of Jesus's words on the cross when He said, "It is finished" (John 19:30).

Another way to talk about the penalty of sin is its *guilt*. We are found guilty. But then, Christ assumes our guilt, paying its penalty so that His blood cleanses us of both sin's power and sin's guilt. Or as the well-known hymn "Rock of Ages" puts it:

> *Let the water and the blood,*
> *From Thy riven side which flowed,*

Be of sin, the double cure,
Cleanse me from its guilt and power.

We have the *double* cure—from sin's guilt and power. What's the effect? There is no more judgment and retributive wrath for believers. There is no more "condemnation for those who are in Christ Jesus" (Rom. 8:1). If God still had some wrath stored up for you, then Jesus didn't fully pay the penalty for your sin. But as it is, God's justice was fully satisfied by the death of His Son. Amazing love! How can it be?

As believers, we still sin. Our "old man," the flesh, still lashes out like a wounded dragon. But it has been dealt the deathblow. It is slowly dying, and God is making your new life in Christ more and more holy. It may not seem like it day to day. But if you look back over the years, you will see the changes. It's like parents marking the stages of growth of their children on a wall or a door frame. It may not seem as though they're growing from day to day, but over time you can see the growth. Even though we find this war raging within our minds and hearts, we ultimately desire God and His will for us.

Paul knew well this inner warfare. He struggled with his heart aflame for God and the sin that still clung closely to him. He wrote:

> I do not understand my own actions. For I do not
> do what I want, but I do the very thing I hate.…
> For I know that nothing good dwells in me, that
> is, in my flesh. For I have the desire to do what is
> right, but not the ability to carry it out. For I do
> not do the good I want, but the evil I do not want

is what I keep on doing. Now if I do what I do not want, it is no longer I who do it, but sin that dwells within me.

So I find it to be a law that when I want to do right, evil lies close at hand. For I delight in the law of God, in my inner being, but I see in my members another law waging war against the law of my mind and making me captive to the law of sin that dwells in my members. (Rom. 7:15, 18–23)

God is killing the old man of sin and causing the new man of righteousness to grow more and more into the likeness of Jesus. This is what we call *sanctification*.

The born-again believer can say, "It is no longer I who live, but Christ who lives in me. And the life I now live in the flesh I live by faith in the Son of God" (Gal. 2:20). God is pleased with us—as His adopted children—not because of our works in unbelief, but because of His work in us. We can cry out to God as our Father because we have the Spirit of adoption in us (Gal. 4:6; Rom. 8:16). This is our new identity.

WHAT ABOUT SMALL SINS?

Why does the least sin deserve death and hell forever? James taught, "Whoever keeps the whole law but fails in one point has become accountable for all of it" (James 2:10). But isn't that a little overboard?

In his book *Follow Me*, David Platt described the seriousness of sin. He argued that the penalty for our sin is not determined by our measure of it. "Instead," he wrote, "the penalty for sin is determined by the magnitude of the one who is sinned against."[3]

If you slapped your friend in the face, what would he or she do? Your friend would probably be confused and might even slap you back. But that would probably be the end of it. However, what if you slapped a police officer? What would happen? You might be charged with assault or be thrown in jail. It's the same act (slapping) but a different consequence.

Now, what if you walked up and slapped the King of Saudi Arabia? Would he simply turn the other cheek? I doubt it. You'd better start pleading for your head!

Apply this concept to sin against a holy, eternal, and sovereign God. Even a "small" sin bears eternal punishment. It's not about the smallness of sin; it's about the greatness and holiness of God. Our view of sin is far too human.

MASKING THE REALITY OF SIN: THREE CONSEQUENCES

When we censor the Scriptures for a feel-good faith—by masking the reality and severity of sin—there are several consequences. First, we won't feel that we actually *deserve* hell, as seen in the previous example. On the other hand, we will believe that we *deserve* health, wealth, and prosperity; that we are good people whose good deeds elicit rewards of material and bodily happiness. Or we believe that God is lucky to have us on His side.

Second, when we mask the reality and depth of our sin, God's justice and judgment against sin "offend" us. We become embarrassed by those passages in Scripture that illustrate God's divine wrath against sin, which offends our modern, man-centered sensitivities. When we read about horrific, even evil, stories in the Bible (see Judg. 19), we should reflect on the seriousness of sin. We should consider its destructive nature. But even those passages of man's sin and God's justice do not compare to the reality of the One who became sin for us on the cross and the divine justice He endured in our place.

Third, when we mask the reality of sin, we mask the need for a Savior. At the end of John Newton's life, already well known for his hymn "Amazing Grace," Newton said, "Although my memory's fading, I remember two things very clearly: I am a great sinner and Christ is a great Savior." When we understand the depth of our sin against a holy and righteous God, we more clearly see our need for Jesus. He didn't wait until we had our act together or until we exhibited enough good deeds to merit His love. No, it was while we were still sinners, guilty of cosmic treason against God, that Christ died for us (Rom. 5:8).

Rather than masking the reality of sin, which exalts man and insults Christ, let us confess it for what it is. Let us unashamedly declare its ugliness and destructive power *so that* the gospel of Jesus might be proclaimed from the rooftops as the good news of great joy for all the people.

TALKING POINTS

Does sin suddenly disappear from our lives when we become Christians? If you think it has in your life, then you will need to start confessing your sin of pride.

While the *presence* of sin hasn't disappeared from our lives, the *power* and *penalty* of sin have been vanquished.

When we understand the depth of our sin against a holy and righteous God, we more clearly see our need for Jesus.

DISCUSSION QUESTIONS

1. Why do you think most self-professing Christians believe we are essentially good by nature? What are some of the reasons for this assumption?

2. How does the Bible describe our preconverted state?

3. Do "small" sins deserve eternal punishment? Why or why not?

9

TURNING A BLIND EYE
TO SUFFERING

When disaster strikes—a deadly tornado, the loss of a child, a school shooting—all we can think about is how to escape the pain. On a national scale, we clamor for answers from panels of religious "experts" to explain the ever-present question, "Why?" We want answers and we want to believe that our suffering isn't meaningless.

Unfortunately, our culture strives to deny the reality of death and suffering, as expressed in our endless pursuit of Botox treatments, anti-aging creams, cosmetic surgeries, and hair dyes. We cloak funerals as "celebrations" and convey the empty promise that all people go to heaven (except perhaps Hitler, Genghis Khan, and Stalin). We can't handle the harsh reality of suffering and so we hide behind the virtual walls of social media, where we pretend our vulnerable hearts are safe from rejection, grief, and the evil "out there." Yet all the while, you and I know it's there, it's real, and it's painful.[1]

The Bible has a lot to say and teach about suffering. Historically, Christians have *prepared* themselves to suffer, knowing that they would face suffering at some point or another. They wanted to be anchored in the whole counsel of God so that when the winds of affliction blew their way, they would remain secure to the Rock of Ages.

LOOKING FOR ANSWERS

Many Christians avoid the topic of suffering altogether. You would be hard pressed to find solid biblical instruction from either the pulpit or the press on the theme of suffering. Many times (if it's discussed at all) it leaves people with more questions than answers. When you experience pain and loss, what do you do? Where do you turn? Is there purpose behind your pain? Is there such a thing as a *sinful* response to suffering, or does the fact that you are suffering justify sinful actions? Can you grow and mature in your faith through suffering?

These are important questions, but it's common to turn a blind eye to suffering—to pretend that the Christian life is all about health, wealth, and prosperity. We're disillusioned when we experience death, pain, and poverty. Certainly, the greatest sufferer, Jesus, has much to teach us.

The irony is that we tend to avoid the topic of suffering, with little to no effort in trying to understand it, thinking that our ignorance-is-bliss utopian world will sustain us when we face affliction. But it backfires. We have nowhere to go and nothing to cling to, and we are rendered functionally hopeless. But this is not God's will for us. He has given us His Word for a purpose, that we might know the truth, love the truth, find rest in the truth, and experience hope by the truth.

We also tend to think that happiness can be found only in the *absence* of suffering. But if you attach happiness and joy to something (or someone) that can crumble or fail, then you are setting yourself up for hopeless despair. However, if you attach your happiness and joy to that which cannot fail—the true and living God—then you can find joy *even in the midst of pain.* Consider Jesus, "who for the joy that was set before him endured the cross" (Heb. 12:2).

You are not spared from the valley of the shadow of death (Ps. 23:4), but as God's child, you are given His comforting presence as you walk through that valley. He is *with* you in the valley because He's been there too. If God is your greatest treasure, you can lose everything and still say, "The LORD gave, and the LORD has taken away; blessed be the name of the LORD" (Job 1:21).

Atheist Richard Dawkins thinks that our suffering is completely meaningless. He wrote, "The total amount of suffering per year in the natural world is beyond all decent contemplation.... Some people are going to get hurt, other people are going to get lucky, and you won't find any rhyme or reason in it." He added, "The universe [is] ... nothing but blind, pitiless indifference."[2] In other words, when we suffer, we are "unlucky." But is suffering truly meaningless? He sounds like another famed atheist, Bertrand Russell, who called the fundamental reality of our lives an "unyielding despair."[3] That'll put wind in our sails.

WHERE DOES SUFFERING COME FROM?

Let's be clear: God did not create suffering during the creation week. On the contrary, He made all things "very good" (Gen. 1:31). He created man—male and female—to live in perfect harmony with Him and with each other. When Adam and Eve chose to rebel against their Maker, God had every right to wipe them from the face of the earth. But He didn't. He graciously promised that One would come to conquer the kingdom of darkness (Gen. 3:15), and God continued His relationship with those made in His image. But despite God's mercy, the curse of their sin remained—suffering.

Adam and Eve's sin brought the fruit of the fall into the world. At the fall, thorns, thistles, disease, and affliction entered creation (Gen. 3:16–19). Even "good" things, such as work and childbearing, would become difficult and painful. Instead of peace and harmony, people began hiding in shame, blaming one another, and hurting one another.

When we suffer today, it should point us to the depth of our sin and the riches of God's grace in saving us through the shed blood of Jesus. But it should also point us back to where suffering began—in Eden. And as we consider the suffering and death brought about through the first Adam, we look to the life and joy brought about through the last Adam (Rom. 5:12–21).

This sin-filled world provided the humble environment of the incarnate God. Jesus humbled Himself and became "obedient to death, even death on a cross" (Phil. 2:8). This would not have been needed or possible if it were not for the fall, which initiated the reality and presence of suffering.

A GOOD AND SOVEREIGN GOD?

Does God ordain suffering? If so, *why*? How is God's sovereignty consistent with His goodness and the reality of suffering in the world? The answers to these questions may not be as difficult as you might think.

Christians can take comfort in the fact that the Scriptures give a sustainable, coherent, helpful, and hopeful understanding of the connection between God's goodness, sovereignty, and omnipresence[4] on the one hand and the reality of suffering on the other. God is good, sovereign, and everywhere at the same time. If any one of these attributes of God is false or lacking, we cannot have a sustainable or consistent biblical view of suffering. Let me explain.

If God is good but not sovereign, then He doesn't have enough control or power to stop suffering. While He might be benevolent and nice, He simply couldn't stop the suffering if He wanted. If God is sovereign but not good, then He is simply a divine bully, wicked and unjust. If God is both sovereign and good but is not everywhere at the same time by His Spirit, then He cannot effectively exert His sovereignty and goodness wherever suffering occurs. Therefore, all three of these divine attributes must be true at the same time for a biblically *consistent* understanding of why and how God ordains suffering.

SUFFERING AND EVIL

Suffering in and of itself is not morally evil. Typically, the two are linked together, but this can lead to a misunderstanding. As we have seen, suffering is the fruit or curse of the fall. Moral evil, on the other hand, is that which rebels against God and His will. Thus, suffering is the *effect and curse* of evil, not evil itself. It would be rather odd for Paul to say, for example, "We rejoice in our sufferings" (Rom. 5:3) if suffering were evil!

Therefore, God can ordain suffering and keep His goodness intact. He doesn't sovereignly create evil. He can ordain suffering, but
He's not the author of sin and evil. So how does God's character con-
nect with the reality of evil in the world? Answer: God permits evil,
restrains evil, and overrules evil for His good and sovereign purposes.
Let's look briefly at these three actions of God in relation to evil by
way of a few biblical examples.

Recall the story of Job in which God asked Satan, "Have you
considered my servant Job?" (Job 1:8). We are told that Job was a
blameless and upright man who feared God and turned away from
evil (v. 8). Satan desired to bring pain and ruin on Job, but he could
exert his malicious intent only by the *permission* of God. God limited
Satan's evil activity by permitting Satan to do harm. Even Satan is on
a sovereign leash. In 2 Corinthians 12, Paul related his "thorn ... in
the flesh" as something intended by God to keep him humble, but
he called it "a messenger of Satan" (v. 7). God permits satanic activity
for much greater purposes.

But God not only permits evil, He also *restrains* evil. For example, we read of Abraham's journey toward the Negeb in Genesis
20. When he and his wife, Sarah, came to the region of Gerar,
Abimelech, the King of Gerar, took notice of Sarah and sought her
as his wife. Abraham lied and told him that she was his sister, and
so Abimelech took her to lay with her. But before he committed
adultery by sleeping with Sarah, God told Abimelech, "You are a
dead man because of the woman whom you have taken, for she is a
man's wife" (v. 3). Abimelech pleaded to God for mercy because he
did not know Sarah was Abraham's wife. So God told Abimelech:
"I know that you have done this in the integrity of your heart, and

it was I who kept you from sinning against me. Therefore I did not let you touch her" (v. 6). God sovereignly restrained further sin and evil for His good purposes. Apart from His common grace in our everyday lives, in restraining sin, we would spin headlong into further self-destruction and suffering.

But God not only permits and restrains evil, He also *overrules* evil for good. One of the clearest examples of this is found in the account of Joseph and his brothers in Genesis. Because of their jealousy of their father's love for Joseph, his brothers sold him into slavery. Potiphar, the captain of Pharaoh's guard, bought Joseph and, over time, made Joseph manager over his house. But Potiphar's wife sought Joseph to lay with her, and one day, while being assaulted by her desires, Joseph ran, leaving his cloak behind in the clutches of the woman. She screamed and lied to Potiphar's men, telling them that Joseph had tried to rape her. So Joseph was thrown into prison.

Through a series of events, Joseph correctly interpreted Pharaoh's dreams and was made second in command over all of Egypt. After seven years of plenty, the region faced seven years of famine. By God's grace, Joseph had ordered extra grain to be saved during the seven years of plenty and so people came from near and far to purchase grain from the Egyptians.

In time, Joseph's brothers also came to purchase grain. After several encounters with his brothers, who didn't recognize him, Joseph finally disclosed his identity. They felt terribly sorry for their actions. But Joseph told them, "As for you, you meant evil against me, but God meant it for good, to bring it about that many people should be kept alive, as they are today" (Gen. 50:20).

While Joseph's brothers meant harm and evil against Joseph, God *overruled* their evil intent, bringing their wicked desires into the fold of His eternal and sovereign purposes. The apostle Paul echoed this when he wrote, "And we know that for those who love God *all things* work together for good, for those who are called according to his purpose" (Rom. 8:28). Because we are finite and our minds are limited as God's created image bearers, we have been given only what we need to know and understand in God's Word. Indeed, "the secret things belong to the LORD our God, but the things that are revealed belong to us and to our children forever" (Deut. 29:29).

While God certainly created both the visible world and the invisible laws of creation (gravity, cause and effect, motion, weather patterns), He doesn't simply let those laws function apart from His immediate and providential governing. In theological language, we call this the doctrine of concurrence, as God concurrently establishes secondary causes in nature and providentially governs them at every second. Hurricanes, forest fires, and deadly floods all occur according to God's sovereign hand. Examples abound in the Scriptures.

Let's take the issue of weather, rain, and thunderstorms. God caused the flood in Noah's day (Gen. 6–8), and He sends the rain on both the just and the unjust (Matt. 5:45). As Elihu proclaimed:

> For to the snow [God] says, "Fall on the earth,"
>   likewise to the downpour, his mighty
>   downpour....
> By the breath of God ice is given,
>   and the broad waters are frozen fast.
> He loads the thick clouds with moisture;

the clouds scatter his lightning.
They turn around and around by his guidance,
to accomplish all that he commands them
on the face of the habitable world.
Whether for correction or for his land
or for love, *he causes it to happen.*
(Job 37:6, 10–13)

Read those last lines again. God *causes* even the seemingly "natural" events to happen "to accomplish all that he commands them on the face of the habitable world." God does not come alongside the secondary laws of nature collaterally. No, the secondary causes of nature exist and function only by the sovereign direction of God— every movement of the clouds, every falling sparrow, every flash of lightning.

WHY DOES GOD ORDAIN SUFFERING?

The Christian church today has all but abandoned a robust and refreshingly biblical theology of suffering.[5] Thus, it would behoove us to consider the voices of the past—in particular the Puritans—those who not only tasted some of the most bitter afflictions to befall humanity but who have also, so skillfully, applied the balm of gospel promise to those who would receive it by faith.

One of the greatest Puritan expositors of a theology of suffering was John Flavel (1630–1691) of Dartmouth, England.[6] Flavel experienced severe suffering within his own lifetime with the loss of three wives, two sons, his parents, ejection from the Church of

England, and the continual persecution from state officials. While God ordains suffering ultimately for His glory, the good of His people, and the judgment of the unbelieving world, here are Flavel's eight answers to the question: Why does God sovereignly ordain suffering *for Christians?*[7]

1. To Reveal, Deter, and Mortify Sin

When afflictions press against a believer, he or she may see his or her true inclinations, which are often full of sin. Flavel wrote, "I heartily wish that these searching afflictions may make the more satisfying discoveries; that you may now see more of the evil of sin, the vanity of the creature, and the fulness of Christ, than ever you yet saw."[8] These "searching afflictions" are meant to reveal sin to the sinner so that it might both deter further wrongdoing *and* so that it might mortify that sin exposed. God will sometimes lay strong afflictions on the body to prevent a worse evil. Flavel contended, "The design and aim of these afflictive providences, is to purge and cleanse them from that pollution into which temptations have plunged them."[9]

2. To Produce Godliness and Spiritual Fruit

Not only does sin need to be removed, but it also needs to be replaced by those things that are pleasing to God. When believers please God by faith-filled good works, they are filled with happiness and bring Him glory. Suffering is the ground from which God brings forth fruit from His people. In this way, suffering is the breeding ground of spiritual fruit so that God, as it were, plants the believer into the soil of suffering to produce godliness.

3. To Reveal More of the Character of God

Another reason God ordains suffering is to reveal His own attributes and character, not objectively, but *experientially* to the suffering believer. God's glory, Flavel maintained, is displayed or illustrated by suffering. Flavel wrote, "By exposing his people to such grievous sufferings, he gives a fit opportunity to manifest the glory of his power ... and of his wisdom."[10] Suffering reveals the glory of God's manifold attributes, which are viewed individually by faith through particular afflictions.

We will often experience God's attributes of wisdom and power in certain afflictions. My mom died when I was fourteen, leaving me with questions and confusion. But over the years, I have come to experience God's greater wisdom and power wrought through her death. I have seen people come to saving faith because of her life testimony, and it has given me an opportunity to empathize with others' suffering.

4. To Relinquish the Temporal for the Eternal

God ordains suffering to loosen the believer's grip on temporal and earthly things. Flavel wrote, "Be careful to ... mortify your inordinate affections to earthly things." Rather, "*exercise heavenly mindedness, and keep your hearts upon things eternal, under all the providences with which the Lord exercises you in this world.*"[11] God has "blessed crosses to mortify corruption ... and to wean us from the world!"[12] Similarly, by these afflictions, we may discover the emptiness and vanity of the world.

5. To Produce a Sincere Faith, Devoid of Hypocrisy

God ordains suffering to produce a sincere faith in the believer, devoid of hypocrisy. But it can also distinguish the believer from the unbeliever. The effect is seen, therefore, in how one *responds* to suffering, as a sort of test. Suffering has a way of clearing out the corruptions of the heart to leave it more faithful and sincere unto God.

6. To Encourage Fellowship with God through the Word, Prayer, and the Sacrament of the Lord's Supper

It is the Christian's joyful duty to develop and cultivate a deeper and more meaningful relationship and fellowship with God—*especially* in times of suffering. Affliction, Flavel argued, "drives them nearer to God, makes them see the necessity of the life of faith, with multitudes of other benefits."[13] Turning to the Word for communing with God is especially important during times of suffering. Affliction also "awakens" the believer to pray more frequently and fervently. Indeed, prayer is one of the best ways for the Christian to ease her heart when overwhelmed by sorrow. Flavel added, "I am sure the sweetest melody of prayer is upon the deep waters of affliction."[14]

God also ordains suffering so as to encourage the believer in Christ to cultivate greater fellowship with Himself through the

sacrament of the Lord's Supper. Flavel saw a direct relationship between the sufferings experienced by Christ—the benefits of which
are represented and sealed in the Lord's Supper to the believer by
faith—and the sufferings experienced by the Christian.

7. To Bear Witness to the World

This witness carries two interwoven strands. First, there is a witness
to the *reality* of the gospel in the believer's life and its call to an unbelieving world to repent and believe in Christ for salvation. Second,
it bears witness *against* those who remain in their unbelief. As God-
honoring responses to suffering bear witness that the Christian faith
is the greatest reality in the world, so also do they demonstrate a full
and living testimony against unbelief.

8. To Cultivate Communion with Christ, the Greatest Sufferer

Finally, God ordains suffering for Christians so that we may commune with Christ, the greatest Sufferer, who suffered on our account.
Not only does Christ know and understand the affliction of His
elect, but also the elect can—in a mystical sense—commune with
Christ because He suffered for them. And one of the best expressions
of the believer's union and communion with Christ comes through
the experience of suffering.

We should prepare ourselves to suffer and to respond in ways
that would glorify God. Unlike the advice of our atheist friends, our
suffering isn't meaningless and your life isn't an "unyielding despair."
The Bible's teaching on the subject of affliction or God's sovereignty

over it shouldn't embarrass us. It may be tempting to censor the Scriptures—only affirming *portions* of what it teaches about God and suffering—but the Word stands by itself. It doesn't need our help. When we honestly observe and consider the suffering and evil around us, the message of the Bible is coherent and hopeful. As you face trials, may you take up your lodgings in the promises of God and say, with Martin Luther:

Let goods and kindred go
This mortal life also
The body they may kill
God's truth abideth still
His kingdom is forever.[15]

TALKING POINTS

Our culture strives to deny the reality of death and suffering, as expressed in our endless pursuit of Botox treatments, anti-aging creams, cosmetic surgeries, and hair dyes.

We can't handle the harsh reality of suffering and so we hide behind the virtual walls of social media, where we pretend our vulnerable hearts are safe from rejection, grief, and the evil "out there."

It is the Christian's joyful duty to develop and cultivate a deeper and more meaningful relationship and fellowship with God—*especially* in times of suffering.

DISCUSSION QUESTIONS

1. What three attributes of God are necessary to keep intact to have a biblically consistent and coherent view of suffering?

2. What's the difference between suffering and evil? Where did suffering come from?

3. Of the eight reasons given for why God ordains suffering for believers, which one strikes you as the most significant? Why?

10

HIDING THE HORRORS OF HELL

Americans are obsessed with heaven, or at least with books about it. I regularly check the bestseller lists to see what people are buying, and I have been amazed by the number of books on heaven lately—*Heaven Is for Real*, *Proof of Heaven*, *90 Minutes in Heaven*, to name a few.

As you might expect, I couldn't find any bestseller on hell. According to a recent poll, only 61 percent of Americans believe that hell is a real place.[1] We don't want to talk about it, read about it, or think about it. It's even considered a bad word in many homes. On the other hand, books that give evangelical Christians an escape of having to affirm the doctrine of hell *do* make the bestseller lists.

Why is this? Why do we obsess with heaven while hiding the horrors of hell? Is it because it's too scary to think about? I doubt it. Americans don't seem to have any problem with horror movies or haunted houses. Professor John Gerstner once said:

The idea of hell that involves some kind of eternal
punishment at the hands of a just and holy God is
so profoundly difficult for us to handle emotionally, that the only person who would have enough
authority to convince us of the reality of such a
place would be Jesus Himself.[2]

In a faith culture that seems to emphasize a watered-down,
nonoffensive approach to the Christian life, we need to recover a
sobering yet unashamed belief in the doctrine and reality of hell.

INVENTING RELIGION

When I was an undergraduate student at Samford University
in Birmingham, Alabama, I had an unofficial debate with Bart
Campolo over lunch. Bart is the son of Tony Campolo, spiritual
adviser to former president Bill Clinton. Bart had just given a
speech at Samford's weekly convocation in which he argued that we
do not need to really tell unbelievers about Jesus; we just need to
"show them love." He was promoting what is oftentimes called the
"social gospel," which basically reduces missions and evangelism
to acts of kindness. It reminds me of the erroneous belief, often
attributed to St. Francis of Assisi, "Preach the gospel. And if you
have to, use words."

In 2014, Bart "left" the Christian faith to be the humanist
chaplain at the University of Southern California. Bart said of his
struggle with Christianity before his departure, "I became very open
about the fact that I would ignore certain Bible verses and underline

others." It sounds a lot like the experience that began to shake me out of my embarrassment of the Bible (see chapter 1).

How did his father respond? Tony wrote, "You know me. I'm not afraid you're going to hell because the God I believe in doesn't send people to hell for eternity for having the wrong theology."[3] It appears that his father was ignoring certain Bible verses as well.

Both Bart and his father have censored the biblical text because they are uncomfortable and embarrassed by what it says. The alternative, a road they have chosen to travel, is to invent a new religion altogether. Either we embrace biblical Christianity—both the good and the offensive—or we invent another religion based on our experiences and feelings. The issue is that our fear of man often outshines our fear of God. But what would happen if you dared to embrace the entire Bible?

WITH FEAR AND TREMBLING

A number of books over the last several years have helped expose this censorship-of-hell epidemic in American religion. Specifically, I'm thinking of *Erasing Hell: What God Said about Eternity, and the Things We've Made Up* by Francis Chan and Preston Sprinkle and *Hell Is Real (But I Hate to Admit It)* by Brian Jones.[4] Both of these are very helpful in shedding light on this trend and what we can do about it.

If we are honest, it's hard to come to grips with the fact that many of our friends, family members, and coworkers will experience the torments of eternal hell because of their unbelief. It's not something we want to talk about, think about, or even study.

But with deep conviction, we must lay our pride down before the wisdom and lordship of God. Our task is not to reinvent religion

but to faithfully pass on the "faith that was once for all delivered to
the saints" (Jude v. 3). And yes, as I attempt to pass this on, I have a
sobering sense of fear and trembling.

After extensive research on what the New Testament has to say
about the topic of hell, Francis Chan concluded:

> The New Testament writers didn't have the same
> allergic reaction to hell as I do. Perhaps they had a
> view of God that is much bigger than mine. A view
> of God that takes Him at His word and doesn't try to
> make Him fit our own moral standards and human
> sentimentality. A view of God that believes what He
> says, even when it doesn't make perfect sense to us.[5]

Chan made a great point. Why do *I* have such an issue with
affirming the doctrine of hell when the New Testament writers spoke
so boldly of it? They, too, had friends and family members who didn't
know Christ. Is it because we live in a hypersensitive, politically correct culture? I'm sure that has something to do with it.

But I can't blame just culture. The truth is, I struggle to affirm
the reality of hell because of my arrogance in believing that I know
better than God and that sin against a thrice-holy God isn't so bad as
to deserve everlasting punishment.

WHAT DOES THE BIBLE ACTUALLY TEACH?

What does Scripture actually teach about hell? While Jesus certainly healed the sick and gave food to the hungry, He also spoke

about hell more than anybody else in the Bible. In Matthew 25, Jesus gave an extended lesson on the final judgment. When He comes again, He will separate His bride, the church, from the unbelieving world—as a shepherd separates sheep from the goats. He will welcome His people but tell those who reject Him: "Depart from me, you cursed, into the eternal fire prepared for the devil and his angels.... And these will go away into eternal punishment, but the righteous into eternal life" (Matt. 25:41, 46). Hell is a place of eternal fire, which God *prepared* for those who reject Him. Let that sink in.

In Matthew 13, Jesus taught, "The Son of Man will send his angels, and they will gather out of his kingdom all causes of sin and all law-breakers, and throw them into the fiery furnace. In that place there will be weeping and gnashing of teeth" (vv. 41–42). So we learn that hell is a place of torment, suffering, and weeping. It's called a "fiery furnace" (v. 50), where unbelievers experience forever the unmitigated wrath of a just and holy God (see also Matt. 18:8). Or as the apostle John explained, it's like a "lake of fire and sulfur ... and they will be tormented day and night forever and ever" (Rev. 20:10). While some have argued a theory of annihilation—that the unbeliever is simply annihilated in hell—the Bible teaches the unending, eternal character of hell.

From my study of Scripture, I see hell being not the complete absence of God's presence, but the absence of His saving and gracious presence. As for His common grace, He causes the sun to shine on the whole world and the rain to fall on the just and the unjust alike (Matt. 5:45). God is everywhere, omnipresent. "If I ascend to heaven, you are there! If I make my bed in Sheol, you are there!"

(Ps. 139:8). Hell, therefore, isn't God's complete absence, but the absence of His gracious presence. It is, rather, the full presence of His unmitigated wrath.

In the Old Testament, we see a similar idea of everlasting life and everlasting death. For example, in the book of Daniel, we read:

> But at that time your people shall be delivered, everyone whose name shall be found written in the book. And many of those who sleep in the dust of the earth shall awake, some to everlasting life, and some to shame and everlasting contempt. (12:1–2)

Isaiah, in looking ahead to "the new heavens and the new earth," spoke of the people who rebelled against God as those who "shall not die [and] their fire shall not be quenched" (Isa. 66:22, 24).

The apostle Paul wrote that when Jesus returns, He will inflict "vengeance on those who do not know God and on those who do not obey the gospel of our Lord Jesus. They will suffer the punishment of eternal destruction" (2 Thess. 1:8–9). Other biblical writers spoke of hell as a place of "eternal fire" (Jude v. 7), a place of "gloomy darkness" (2 Pet. 2:4), a place of "torment" (Luke 16:23), and a "hell of fire" (Matt. 5:22).

Will some suffer worse than others? The Scriptures do seem to teach that, as there are varying degrees of reward in heaven, so also there are varying degrees of punishment and pain in hell (see Matt. 11:21–24; Luke 12:42–48; 16:1–9; 20:47; Rom. 2:4–9).

JESUS, THE ONLY WAY?

The exclusivity of Jesus—that He's the only way to heaven—could have been an entire chapter in this book. It is one of the most controversial and censored Bible truths in our day. As we saw in Paul's instruction from 2 Thessalonians 1, there will be "vengeance on those who do not know God and on those who do not obey the gospel of our Lord Jesus" (v. 8). Will those who do not know and obey Jesus experience the everlasting torments of hell?

With fear and trembling, we must confess, yes.

Peter taught, "There is salvation in no one else, for there is no other name under heaven given among men by which we must be saved" (Acts 4:12). Paul wrote, "There is ... one Lord, one faith, one baptism" (Eph. 4:4–5). Jesus Himself said, "I am the way, and the truth, and the life. No one comes to the Father except through me" (John 14:6). Note these last words: "No one comes to the Father." If Jesus had left it at that, there would be no good news. However, Jesus gave *one exception*: those who come through Him. That is, those who believe that He is the Christ, the Son of God, and Savior of sinners (20:31).

Sometimes people will give an illustration of blind men and an elephant to show that all "paths" lead to God. In the illustration, several blind men happen upon an elephant. They each grab hold of a different part of the elephant and begin describing it as they feel. The man who grabs hold of the elephant's ear says, "An elephant is large and flat." The man who grabs hold of the elephant's trunk remarks, "No, the elephant is long and muscular." You get the idea.

The point of the illustration is that we are all blind men in our religious convictions, all having *some* element of truth. The Muslim, the Jew, the Buddhist, and the Christian are describing the same god and, therefore, all of those paths lead to the same god. However, this illustration comes with an Achilles' heel. In his book *The Reason for God*, Tim Keller explained this story and argued:

> The story is told from the point of view of someone who is not blind. How could you know that each blind man only sees part of the elephant unless *you* claim to be able to see the whole elephant? …
>
> How could you possibly know that no religion can see the whole truth unless you yourself have the superior, comprehensive knowledge of spiritual reality you just claimed that none of the religions have?[6]

As soon as you begin saying that all religions are the same, either you don't know what you're talking about or you are claiming an arrogantly superior perspective with no foundation.

What about those who have never heard the gospel? What about the poor native in Africa or the Eskimo in northern Canada? Certainly they won't go to hell if they've never heard the gospel, right? But the reason we engage in missions is precisely because the Bible teaches that *all* are lost apart from the saving knowledge of God in Christ.

Can God save them in a way that is outside of His ordinary means of drawing people into a saving relationship with Himself? Absolutely. But He has revealed that He saves through the preaching of the gospel. Faith comes by hearing the word of Christ (Rom.

10:17). That is God's design for gathering His people. If our evangelism suddenly put people in a position of going to hell—*because* they have heard the gospel—then we should never engage in evangelism.

Moreover, there are no "innocent" people in Africa, Canada, Australia, or America. "None is righteous, no, not one … for all have sinned and fall short of the glory of God" (Rom. 3:10, 23). People have been given enough revelation of the presence and power of God to render them "without excuse" (1:20). Again, these are offensive and difficult words to hear, especially with our postmodern ears. But this is the Bible uncensored.

DID JESUS "DESCEND" INTO HELL?

In the Apostles' Creed, we read the words "and he descended into hell." What does it mean that Jesus "descended" into hell? To be sure, the phrase is not found in any of the early versions of the Creed, nor does it appear in the Bible. Jesus told the thief on the cross, "Today you will be with me in Paradise" (Luke 23:43). Moreover, when Christ cried out, "It is finished!" it would be difficult to reconcile that with three more days in hell (John 19:30).

John Calvin took the phrase to mean that Christ suffered the pains of hell while on the cross.[7] The Heidelberg Catechism (1563) sees in this phrase the idea of Christ being "plunged" into the depths of suffering (Q44). The Westminster Larger Catechism (1647) understands the phrase to mean that Christ was buried and in the state of the dead until the third day (Q50). Christ, therefore, did not descend into hell for three days but rather *experienced* hell—in all of its fullness—on the cross *and* remained in the state of bodily death until the third day.[8]

FACING OUR FEAR

At this, you might be tempted to put this book down. But we must ask *why* the reality of hell was such an important doctrine for Jesus and His disciples to teach. The apostle Paul wrote to young Timothy:

> If you put these things before the brothers, you will be a good servant of Christ Jesus, being trained in the words of the faith and of the good doctrine that you have followed....
>
> Keep a close watch on yourself and on the teaching. Persist in this, for by so doing you will save both yourself and your hearers. (1 Tim. 4:6, 16)

We are to keep a "close watch" on our teaching and doctrine. As we've seen, the doctrine of hell is important. And while it may be difficult to think about emotionally, we shouldn't dismiss it as an insignificant, unimportant reality. As Brian Jones wrote in *Hell Is Real (But I Hate to Admit It)*, "The Bible says in 2 Timothy 3:16, 'All Scripture is God-breathed.' All of it—not just the parts we like, but every single command."[9]

The reality of hell should point us to the reality and heinousness of sin. We *deserve* hell and death forever, all of us. But Jesus experienced our hell on the cross so that, for those who trust in Him for salvation and life, there is no more hell to pay. However, for those who continue to reject Him—those who remain fixed in their rebellion against His grace in the gospel—they will not experience His salvation. Rather, they will experience hell forever.

Today is the day of salvation (2 Cor. 6:2). You never know when your time on earth will come to an end. Our lives are like a fleeting breath—"a mist that appears for a little time and then vanishes" (James 4:14). There will be no second chance, as we learn from the story of the rich man and Lazarus in Luke 16. Jesus taught, "Whatever you bind on earth shall be bound in heaven, and whatever you loose on earth shall be loosed in heaven" (Matt. 18:18). So *today* is the day of salvation. Run to Jesus, whose death sets you free from bondage to sin and secures your hope with Him forever.

TALKING POINTS

We don't want to talk about hell, read about it, or think about it. It's even considered a bad word in many homes.

In a faith culture that seems to emphasize a watered-down, nonoffensive approach to the Christian life, we need to recover a sobering yet unashamed belief in the doctrine and reality of hell.

Either we embrace biblical Christianity—both the good and the offensive—or we invent another religion based on our experiences and feelings.

DISCUSSION QUESTIONS

1. Why do you think books about heaven are bestsellers but books about hell are hard to come by?

2. Why do you think Jesus and His disciples taught so much about hell? What should that teach us today?

3. What does God's call for us to evangelize and engage in missions tell us about the state of people in unreached parts of the world?

11

GOING AFTER GIMMICKS: "SUCCESS" IN THE ENTERTAINMENT CHURCH

As the bass drum rattled my insides, cannons shot confetti over the sea of cheering fans. "Are you ready to worship?" yelled a twenty-something hipster from center stage. Christian lyrics to Lady Gaga music graced the screens up front, and off we went, though I found myself still reeling from the previous series of skits, which were hil-*ar*-ious![1]

A verse was read from some *relevant, nonoffensive, gender-neutral version* of the Bible and that's the last I heard of it. The rest of the "sermon" was brimming with anecdotes and heartwarming stories.

Whatever we were doing that Sunday morning (worship?), one thing was certain: I was witnessing the greatest show on earth—complete with circulating lights, fog machines, artistic backgrounds, and dueling DJs. I almost missed the Communion stations that outlined the perimeter of the assembly for anyone who wanted to partake when the Spirit "moved them" to do so.

EMBARRASSED TO FAIL

Nobody likes to fail, and pastors and ministry leaders are no exception. I think sometimes the reason the church so often resorts to all kinds of gimmicks to attract people is because we somehow believe we are helping out God. Maybe He needs a little assistance and a real-world marketing strategy.

Unfortunately, the question we often ask is, "What can I do to get people to come to church?" Instead, our question *should be*, "What is God's design for the church, worship, and ministry?"

We should go to the Scriptures to understand, for example, God's will for corporate worship or how we should disciple the next generation. How can the Bible better inform and regulate our worship and ministry? Do you see a lot of church gimmicks today that would be completely foreign to Jesus and His disciples?

Because we are embarrassed to fail in ministry, we become embarrassed by the simplicity of God's design for the church. If we really believe that God uses the basic, apostolic means of saving and sanctifying His people, why do we feel the need to invent a Hollywood-style, entertainment-driven, and success-oriented ministry?

Jesus will build His church, and He uses us to do it. But the "church" many are building across America and around the world hardly resembles the instruction for worship and ministry we find in the pages of Scripture. Rather than censoring the Bible's guidance on these things, we should do everything to investigate and study and understand what God's design truly is. I want to show you why.

ENTERTAINMENT—THE NEW NORMAL

Following America's lead, churches around the globe are spending through the roof trying to attract the greatest number of people into their worship gatherings. Success is the name of the church-growth game. "Whatever it takes to get them in the doors," one older pastor recently told me. "People just want to be real and to be accepted for who they are. And that's what we do in worship."

The trend of making worship and ministry entertainment driven is certainly nothing new, but it is becoming the new *normal*. From "Christian" magicians and bodybuilders to skit guys and shock-factor eating contests, from piano drops (yes, dropping a piano from a crane onto a parking lot) to iPad giveaways, churches across America are using gimmicks to scale the heights of ministry success. And who doesn't want large numbers flocking to their stadiums chanting Christian slogans that one might see on a bumper sticker? It makes you feel good.

I attended a parachurch organization's weekly youth "Ignite" meeting (or some similar name that was invariably filled with all sorts of entertaining gimmicks). Again, I could have guessed the rationale: "We only do these things to get them in the door," the speaker explained later to me. "Then we tell them about Jesus." Sneaky.

If you are thinking about charting this course of a "do whatever it takes" approach to ministry and worship, please consider this axiom:

you keep them by how you attract them. If people are coming to your church because of your funny, lighthearted stories, you had better not stop, because they will leave. If you've attracted teenagers into your congregation through your rock-star worship leader, you had better not let him go. Ironically, those who have told me that they do these stunts only to get people in the door *never stop*. What begins as an evangelism tactic quickly becomes a regular method of ministry.

FAITHFULNESS OVER SUCCESS

Pastors and church leaders are constantly battling the pressure of ministry success from other staff and members, competition with the big church down the road, and the ever-present drive to "engage" the culture. In fact, one of the most frequent questions a pastor receives is, "How many did you have in worship?" or "How big is your church?" It seems like buildings, bodies, and budgets sideline Christ crucified, a stumbling block and offense. But is this approach the kind of worship and ministry our God has prescribed? Does God not also care about our *method*?

In their book *Liberating Ministry from the Success Syndrome*, Kent and Barbara Hughes argue that it is always better to be faithful to the Lord than successful in ministry. God is sovereign, but *our* task is to faithfully plant and water the gospel of Jesus Christ—looking to *Him* to provide the growth (1 Cor. 3:7). It is the Spirit who gives life; the flesh is of no avail (John 6:63). "For apart from me," Jesus says, "you can do nothing" (15:5).

Faithfulness to God in both content and method—not success—is our chief aim.

Even though some today are pushing for a theology of "fruitfulness" in ministry, on a *functional* level, there is little difference from the success-driven model so prevalent in churches today. God has called you to be faithful to Him and has given guidance in His Word for both worship and ministry.

THE SUFFICIENCY OF SCRIPTURE

If there is something called "acceptable worship" (Heb. 12:28), there must also be *un*acceptable worship. Nadab and Abihu quickly learned this lesson by offering "unauthorized fire" before the Lord (Lev. 10:1–2). God told post-exilic Israel in their halfhearted worship inventions, "Oh that there were one among you who would shut the doors, that you might not kindle fire on my altar in vain!" (Mal. 1:10). When we have prioritized ministry success as our goal, we light useless fires.

While God has given some liberty in the structure of worship, the place of worship, and so on (see John 4:21–24), we are not left without prescription and biblical guidance. The central question remains: Is God's Word *sufficient* to guide us in both the content of our worship and ministries and the means by which we go about them? Absolutely. The problem lies not with the Word, but with our man-made inventions.

MINISTRY BY THE MEANS OF GRACE

The wonderful truth is that God has not left us in the dark on these matters. He has given His church the means by which *He*, the eternal and sovereign God, both saves and sanctifies His people. Thus, God cares about not only what we teach and preach in our ministry but also the way we go about it, our methodology.

I maintain that the how-to of being faithful to God in worship and ministry is demonstrated through the ordinary, historic, and apostolic *means of grace*—particularly, ministry of the Word, prayer, and sacraments, though you could also include gospel-motivated service and grace-centered community. They're not fancy or hip, and they certainly won't land you on the big stage of *Your Best Life Now*! But together, these five ordinances of Christ are the basic means by which God saves and grows His people.

We find these together, for example, in Acts 2:42–47. The early disciples "devoted themselves" to five things: the Word, fellowship, the Lord's Supper, prayer, and service. The result: "And the Lord added to their number day by day those who were being saved" (v. 47). The Gentiles, upon hearing the preaching of Paul and Barnabas at Antioch in Pisidia, "began rejoicing and glorifying the word of the Lord, and as many as were appointed to eternal life believed" (13:48). They preached; God saved.

Historic creeds and confessions have also understood ministry and worship by the means of grace. For example, the Westminster Larger Catechism (1647), question 154, asks: "What are the outward means whereby Christ communicates to us the benefits of his mediation?" Answer: "The outward and ordinary means whereby Christ communicates to his church the benefits of his mediation are all his ordinances; especially the Word, sacraments, and prayer; all of which are made effectual to the elect for their salvation."

The London Baptist Confession of Faith (1689) likewise maintains, "The grace of faith … is increased and strengthened by the work of the Spirit through the ministry of the Word, and also by the administration of baptism and the Lord's Supper, prayer, and other means appointed by God" (14.1). In other words, God has provided the ordinary means by which He both saves and sanctifies His people.

These means of grace do not work *ex opere operato* ("from the work worked"), as Roman Catholic theology contends; they do not function like a magical formula of cause and effect. For example, preaching God's Word on a particular Sunday morning does not *necessarily* mean that every unbeliever who listens will surely come to saving faith, nor does it mean that every Christian will surely grow in his or her faith that day. Rather, God works in and through the means of grace as He sees fit for the building up of His church. His Word will not return to Him empty but will accomplish His purpose for it (Isa. 55:11).

If God has already provided the ordinary means of growing in grace as we find in His Word, why do we think we have the right or the greater wisdom to invent new ways through entertainment-driven, success-oriented worship and ministry?

PUTTING IT TOGETHER

This will no doubt be hard work and, for some, a foundational shift. John Piper explained in *When the Darkness Will Not Lift*, "We find ourselves not energized for any great cause, but always thinking about the way to maximize our leisure and escape pressure."[2] The great irony is that we are "bored" in church *because* we maximize leisure and escape pressure. We are living from one pleasure high to the next, looking for the next big wave to take us closer and closer to the sunny sands of the American Dream. However, the easy road of entertainment and the pursuit of the American Dream have, in the end, left us still bored and still dreaming.

So what might a means-of-grace ministry look like? Let me give you some practical takeaways:

God's Word. Ministry of the Word would include expository preaching (preferably *lectio continua*, "continual reading"), teaching, meditating, and memorizing Scripture. Are these regular ministries of your church? Are you encouraging families to worship together and study the Scriptures together? Are the people in your church *preparing* themselves to hear God's Word preached, even on Saturday night? We do these things because we still believe that "faith comes from hearing, and hearing through the word of Christ" (Rom. 10:17). God's Word—not entertaining stories, skits, or piano drops—is the primary means by which God saves and grows His people.

Prayer. The world, the flesh, and the devil are waging an all-out assault on prayer. Busyness squeezes out what's deemed impractical and elevates the pragmatic. What weak faith we have. A church member recently asked me, "Does prayer change things?" My answer: "No. *God* changes things, but He uses prayer to do it." Prayer is a means by which God accomplishes His purposes and a means of grace by which He strengthens His people by drawing them into greater fellowship with Himself.

A ministry of prayer would include prayer as worship, prayer in large groups, prayer in small groups, prayer as families, and an intentional effort by church leaders to highlight both the delight and duty of regular prayer for individuals. I have found that many adult Christians have a harder time praying out loud than young children. Why? Because we are not in regular prayer ourselves, and church leaders do not highlight the importance of prayer as a biblical means of growing in God's grace.

Sacraments. According to Nielsen reports, the average American spends roughly 3.5 hours a day watching television. That's *in addition* to other forms of media—game consoles, smartphones, movies, and the Internet—all vying for our time and attention. YouTube continues to explode with viral videos from the global community, at times drawing millions of views overnight. Because we are stimulated and energized *visually*, television and movies have dominated the attention and affection of our hearts, and churches have jumped on the (so-called) bandwagon. Churches have often tried to dovetail their ministries with the luster and lure of the entertainment culture. But they simply cannot compete, nor *should* they!

In reality, Hollywood has nothing on the joy, pleasure, truth, and experience found in God's glorious gospel—made visible and effectual through the signs and seals of His covenant of grace. The Bible calls these baptism and the Lord's Supper, and they are means by which God matures His people in the faith. When we witness a baptism, we are to be reminded of our own baptism, that we've been "marked off" from the world, washed by the blood of Christ, and set apart for God in His covenant community. When we partake of the Lord's Supper, we are not merely thinking about Jesus. No, Christ is spiritually and truly present, mysteriously working by His Spirit in His Supper to nourish His people.

Gospel-Motivated Service. Service is a means of grace whereby God grows our faith, reveals our sin, extends our love, and brings us joy and peace. The apostle Paul wrote in Ephesians 4:12 that God has given various gifts to His church "to equip the saints for the work of ministry, for building up the body of Christ." The great example, of course, is Jesus Himself, who said, "For even the Son of Man came not to be served but to serve, and to give his life as a ransom for many" (Mark 10:45). God communicates grace through the means of serving one another and ministering to the brokenness of this world.

The kingdom Jesus inaugurated is a "backward kingdom" in which we die to live, give to receive, and are exalted through humility. Indeed, the gospel we preach is "foolishness" in the eyes of the world (1 Cor. 1:18–25). Our giving of money, time, and gifts should be in response to God's grace in giving His one and only Son. Thus, we never move past the gospel in our service—it should always inform and motivate our serving. Jesus's redemptive work should continually shape and mold our desires to such sufficient intensity that it translates into serving action.[3]

Grace-Centered Community. It is popular in our day to disregard the local church in favor of some purple-haired "prophetess" on TV spewing "heath, wealth, and prosperity." But God has given the body of Christ, displayed in the local church, as the context in which real sin is offered real forgiveness and where we "stir up one another to love and good works" (Heb. 10:24).

Within the community of faith, we are called to confess sin to one another and to pray for one another that we may be healed (James 5:16). As iron sharpens iron, so we exhort one another toward holy living (Prov. 27:17). Moreover, the members of the "body of Christ" are given gifts for the building up of the body. These gifts, as Paul explained, are given by grace as a means by which God grows His church and equips her for greater ministry (Eph. 4:7). Moreover, the unity of this community of faith is the direct result of our union with Christ. Jesus prayed that the church "may all be one, just as you, Father, are in me, and I in you, that they also may be in us" (John 17:21).

With all my heart, I plead with you not to be tempted with success, professionalism, or the fading fads of our entertainment-driven culture. Rather, pursue Jesus as the all-satisfying treasure that He is and strive to faithfully feed His sheep through the means of grace that God has already provided His church. Dare to embrace the entire Bible, which is sufficient for worship and ministry.

TALKING POINTS

Sometimes the reason the church so often resorts to all kinds of gimmicks to attract people is because we somehow believe we are helping out God.

From "Christian" magicians and bodybuilders to skit guys and shock-factor eating contests, churches across America are using gimmicks to scale the heights of ministry success.

We are living from one pleasure high to the next, looking for the next big wave to take us closer and closer to the sunny sands of the American Dream.

DISCUSSION QUESTIONS

1. In ministry, do the ends always justify the means? Or does God also care about the how of our ministry methods?

2. How does knowing that God has called you to faithfulness over success free you from the "success syndrome"?

3. What are the basic, apostolic means by which God both saves and grows His people?

12

DON'T TRY THIS AT HOME: OUTSOURCING PARENTING

I love frying turkeys every Thanksgiving. Each year, my family and friends descend on our home to enjoy the taste of a juicy, peanut-oiled, crispy fried turkey. If you do a web search for fried turkey videos, you will inevitably stumble onto some guy yelling to his friends, "Hey, watch this!" just before he drops a fifteen-pound turkey into the fryer. What he soon discovers is that hot oil and water don't mix. They explode. In similar videos, you may find a group of guys—it's always a group of guys—"experimenting" with exploding turkeys. And out of common courtesy, one of them will look at the camera and say, "Don't try this at home." Good advice.

While exploding a turkey is not recommended, it seems as though biblical parenting has been given the same counsel—"Don't try this at home." More than ever, we are *outsourcing* parenting to swim instructors, soccer coaches, youth pastors, math tutors, and the government. From early morning FCA breakfasts to late-night football practice, and everything in between, parents are abdicating their privilege and responsibility of bringing up their children in the instruction and admonition of the Lord.

According to one estimate, fathers spend less than thirty minutes *a week* talking with their children. When it comes to actual instruction or discipleship, it's practically nonexistent.[1] The overwhelming majority of instruction children receive comes primarily from four avenues: TV, the Internet, their peers, and government education. We would be fools to believe that these do not have a profound impact on shaping their worldviews.

Jesus said, "A disciple is not above his teacher, but everyone when he is fully trained will be like his teacher" (Luke 6:40). Who is your child's "teacher"? When our children are fully trained, they will be like their teachers. More often than not, their teachers are postmodern skeptics and anti-Christian critics. Why are we so confused, then, when our children walk away from the faith—a faith we *thought* they were raised in? Should we really be so surprised when we hear that roughly 70 percent of churchgoing teenagers leave the church by the end of their first year in college?

At the root of this parental outsourcing is a functional embarrassment of what the Bible has to say about Christian parenting. Parents don't want to hear that they have work to do. As soon as a baby is born, we have a proclivity to put them in everything—child care, day care, grandparents' care—everything but our own care. We don't like the fact that raising children takes time, emotional vulnerability, and spiritual investment.

So where do we begin?

BIBLICAL MANHOOD AND WOMANHOOD

My wife and I tend to view Valentine's Day cards as rather cheesy, as if the holiday is my one chance to tell my bride that I love her each year. But out of some mysterious sense of patriotic responsibility, we get cards for each other anyway. Because getting a card isn't exactly on the top of my list, I usually don't make it to the store until February 13. By this point, however, most of the "good" Valentine's Day cards are gone. A few song-playing cards (albeit with fading battery life) and flower cards are all that remain.

But I've noticed a disturbing trend. The next time you are searching for a Valentine's Day or a Mother's Day card, ask yourself, *How are the men typically portrayed on the cards?* It doesn't take long to notice that they are portrayed as buffoons—sitting on the couch, drinking cheap beer, and passing gas while their wives are cleaning or taking care of the children. The same is true in TV sitcoms.

But rather than striving to change this perception in the American mind, we acquiesce and form fit the mold out of a sense of semi-manly duty. We laugh at the similarity between our lives and the stereotype, while our children suffer the consequences.

As the persons of the Trinity are equal in power and glory but have differing roles, so we who are created in His image are equal in dignity, value, and worth but created with differing complementary roles.[2] According to John Piper, the heart of biblical *masculinity* "is a sense of benevolent responsibility to lead, provide for and protect women in ways appropriate to a man's differing relationships." The heart of biblical *femininity*, he added, "is a freeing disposition to affirm, receive and nurture strength and leadership from worthy men in ways appropriate to a woman's differing relationships."[3]

Because of the progress of the feminist agenda and an increasing confusion over what it means to be a man or a woman, we've become functionally ashamed of the Bible's teaching in this area. We don't want to be called a bigot, regressive, or any other socially despicable label.

In a marriage, a husband is called to be the "head" of his wife (1 Cor. 11:3; Eph. 5:22–23). Piper, again, provided some helpful definitions. *Headship*, simply defined, is the "divine calling of a husband to take primary responsibility for Christ-like, servant leadership, protection, and provision in the home." The wife is called to submit to her husband and respect his leadership in the home, as a supporter and helpmate. *Submission*, simply defined, is the "divine calling of a wife to honor and affirm her husband's leadership and help carry it through according to her gifts."[4]

The fall twisted this good creation order so that now the husband will oftentimes be *either* completely passive *or* brutally overbearing. The wife will oftentimes usurp his God-given leadership through manipulation or cynicism. Both are warped expressions of God's design for men and women. Ultimately, marriage is meant to point us to the redemptive image of the church as the bride of Christ (Eph. 5:25–33).

DESPISING CHILDREN

As parents, we have the privilege of investing our lives, our love, and our faith in the next generation. But this is not the way our culture views either parenting or children. Today, children are seen as an inconvenience, another mouth to feed. This is why abortion is even an issue. A couple would rather end a life than invest their own.

It's also why the birthrate in our country is dismal. In 2014, *The Washington Times* reported that the birthrate in the United States had plummeted to a record low, a mere 1.86 percent.[5] A nation needs at least 2.1 percent to be self-sustaining and self-propagating. When compared to the number of births in predominately Muslim-controlled nations—where the rate can reach 6 or 7 percent—our world is becoming Muslim simply through birthrate alone.

But according to Scripture, children are a blessing from the Lord (Ps. 128:3–4) and parents are called to be good stewards of this blessing. We are *not* to look to culture on how to raise children, but to God in His Word. This seems so basic and so elementary for a believing parent to do, but it is one of the most neglected responsibilities of the Christian life.

Douglas Wilson, in his book *Father Hunger*, argued that we have become a "fatherless nation": in the home, in the church, and in the nation.[6] In my years of working in youth ministry, I learned the lasting importance of a father in the home. You cannot replace the pivotal, securing, and caring impact of a loving father.

According to a recent US Census Bureau survey, nearly 40 percent of children in America are raised in single-parent homes—overwhelmingly raised by a single mother (more than 80 percent).[7] Alarmingly, 67 percent of African American children grow up in single-parent homes.[8] And yes, we are experiencing a cultural shift. The number of children living in single-parent homes has nearly doubled in the last fifty years.[9]

In August 2014, a white policeman shot and killed an African American teenager in Ferguson, Missouri. Riots broke out immediately and only escalated when the grand jury didn't indict the policeman. It seemed as though the entire nation took sides, digging in their proverbial heels.

A few months later, on November 26, African American pastor Voddie Baucham published an article on The Gospel Coalition's website, in which he wrote:

> I do believe there are systemic issues plaguing black men. These issues are violence, criminality, and immorality, to name a few. And all of these issues are rooted in and connected to the epidemic of fatherlessness....
>
> We know that fatherlessness is the number one indicator of future violence, dropout rates, out-of-wedlock births, and future incarceration. And in the black community, more than 70 percent of all children are born out of wedlock! Fatherlessness is the bane of the black community.[10]

Wilson and Baucham are right on target: we are a fatherless nation. Where are men who are willing to sacrifice, who love their wives, and who are not ashamed to lead with humility and boldness? More and more, the government is filling the void once occupied by fathers and parents. MSNBC's Melissa Harris-Perry has argued for a socialist understanding of parenting: "We need a collective notion that these are *our* children ... We have to break through this private idea that kids belong to their parents or kids belong to their families."[11] But this is antithetical to a biblical worldview.

THE PRIVILEGE OF PARENTING

Children are a blessing, not an inconvenience. In the Psalms we read, "Like arrows in the hand of a warrior are the children of one's youth. Blessed is the man who fills his quiver with them!" (127:4–5). We also find, "Your wife will be like a fruitful vine within your house; your children will be like olive shoots around your table. Behold, thus shall the man be blessed who fears the LORD" (128:3–4). We are His stewards of His many blessings, whether those blessings are money, time, or talents. Children are also a blessing from the Lord, and we have a loving responsibility to search the Scriptures on how to raise them for His glory.

Deuteronomy 6 is one of the most helpful passages on how to raise children. In this well-known text we read:

> You shall love the LORD your God with all your heart and with all your soul and with all your might. And these words that I command you today shall be on your heart. You shall teach them diligently to your children, and shall talk of them when you sit in your house, and when you walk by the way, and when you lie down, and when you rise. (vv. 5–7)

Notice that God's Word is to be in *your heart*, as the parent. The greatest thing your child needs from you is your love for and worship of God. Before we teach these things to our children, they need to be in *our* hearts. We can't give away what we don't have. Moreover, we should teach our children *diligently*—intentionally as those who are fulfilling our God-given responsibility. Finally, we should teach them *at all times*—when we sit, walk, lie down, and rise.

We see a New Testament parallel in Ephesians, which exhorts fathers to "bring [their children] up in the discipline and instruction of the Lord" (6:4). There's no way around this. The primary responsibility of our children's education does not fall on our president, the local baseball coach, or the youth pastor. The primary responsibility of our children's education falls on the parents. We have listened to culture on how to raise children and not to God.

What are some practical implications of this? First, teach your children gender identity, not gender confusion. Raise boys to be men—as leaders, husbands, and fathers. Raise girls to be women, wives, and mothers. I'm not suggesting that women shouldn't work. My wife is a nurse. But I am suggesting that our home life should conform to the uncensored biblical text.

Today, parents spend through the roof preparing their child to get into the right college. They will move to a new location and bend over backward to ensure their son or daughter is president of the school club. They will drive their teenager back and forth to as many school and sporting functions as possible for the potential of a scholarship. But how much are we preparing our children to be good husbands, wives, fathers, and mothers? How much time are we spending to equip them to be faithful servants, using their gifts in the local church?

Next, be present in your children's lives. When people retire, you might hear them say something to the effect of "I'm excited to be able to spend more time with my family now." These are the same people who have spent little to no time with their children for forty years. Now, at the age of sixty or seventy, they want to invest in their children? They should be saying that at the age of twenty or twenty-five. We cannot afford to sacrifice family on the altar of professionalism, success, and bigger paychecks.

UNITING CHURCH AND HOME

I believe that God has created the church and the family as complementary institutions, designed to function together and support each other. At my church, we have a multigenerational vision of being a family-supporting, family-integrated church in which parents and grandparents are being affirmed, equipped, and encouraged to fulfill their God-given privilege and responsibility of bringing up their children in the nurture and instruction of the Lord. We want to see the next generation discipled every day in their homes, not just once a week in church.

We see the impact of Paul's ministry with Timothy. Timothy had followed his mentor's teaching and example, and Paul encouraged young Timothy to "continue in" what he'd learned. Paul wrote, "Continue in what you have learned and have firmly believed, knowing from whom you learned it and how from childhood you have been acquainted with the sacred writings, which are able to make you wise for salvation through faith in Christ Jesus" (2 Tim. 3:14–15).

Timothy was to continue in what he had learned from *both* Paul *and* his family ("whom" is plural). He didn't learn just from the "professional" Christian but also from his parents and grandparents—Lois and Eunice, respectively (2 Tim. 1:5). Timothy had been *acquainted* with the "sacred writings," what we call the Old Testament. And these sacred writings were able to make him wise for "salvation through faith in Christ Jesus." We see the importance of Timothy's upbringing—in which he had become acquainted with God's Word—and the ongoing discipleship of his mentor, Paul.

Similarly, in Titus 2, we see how older men are to disciple younger men and older women are to disciple younger women. However, the context is *not* older men and women with young children or teenagers (like a youth group), but older men and women mentoring younger men and women who are married with children. It's the parents' privilege and responsibility to disciple their children. What might this look like? What could you do? Mentor a younger man or woman. Affirm and encourage parents in their role. In the pew, help younger families, as you are able. Teach them to open their Bibles, learn the songs, and understand biblical giving of tithes and offerings.

Children's and youth directors have been and are currently replacing parents as the primary source of biblical instruction, thus turning the hearts of the children, not to the parents, but to the "professionals" (see Mal. 4:6). In turn, parents are abdicating their God-given responsibility in the home. Please don't misunderstand me. We have a children's director at our church. But her job isn't to *replace* the parents' responsibility; her job is to come alongside parents to equip, train, teach, resource, and pray for them. And she does this under the oversight and leadership of our elders.

If we were to simply let the Bible inform and direct our structure of ministry in the church and at home (sufficiency of Scripture), we wouldn't come up with much of the age-segregated model that we see so often in the church today. This raises the question: Where do you go in the Bible to find justification or any theological, foundational principle for the modern youth and children's ministry programs that are so separated and disconnected from the primary role of the parents? I know of many churches that don't even *allow* children to be with their parents in worship. We are censoring the biblical text.

After a student's graduation from high school or college, *at no other time* are these children segregated by age. They are suddenly turned out on their own, supposedly with the knowledge of how to interact and respect older generations and model character and biblical maturity to younger generations *when they've never done that in school or in church before.*

VISION DISTINCTIVES

I want to close by giving you five vision distinctives of what this might look like in your local church and home life. I will include a list of Bible passages at the end of each distinctive for you to look up on your own.

First, from Scripture, I envision husbands and fathers taking the *primary lead* in discipling their families in the Lord and using their God-given gift of loving responsibility to invest their lives, their love, and their faith in the next generation. This is done through teaching, family worship, catechism, and overall discipline and instruction. To this end, I envision equipping and affirming men to be servant-leaders in their homes—providing for, protecting, nourishing, and cherishing their families (Deut. 6:5–7; Ps. 78:4–7; Prov. 22:6; Mal. 4:6; 1 Cor. 14:33–35; Eph. 6:4; 1 Tim. 2:11–12; 3:4, 12; 2 Tim. 3:15).

Second, I envision individuals and families submitting themselves to the leadership of the local church, studying the truth of Scripture, being present and engaged in worship, and intentionally being a vibrant source of service, encouragement, and ministry to others (1 Tim. 5:17; Titus 1:10–11; Heb. 13:17; 1 Pet. 5:1–5).

Third, I envision children, young and old, being with their parents in Lord's Day (Sunday) worship. I want to equip and encourage families with both young and old children to worship together. Yes, children will make noises, but we should be delighted to have children worshipping with us. If a child continues to be fussy, then you may want to consider having a "cry room" to recover (Deut. 31:12–13; Josh. 8:35; 2 Chron. 20:13; Ezra 10:1; Neh. 12:43; Ps. 148:12–13; Matt. 19:13–14; Mark 9:36; 10:13–16; Luke 18:15–17; Eph. 6:1–2; Col. 3:20).

Fourth, I envision reaching out with the gospel of Jesus Christ to orphans and to other children and youth from either broken homes or homes with unbelieving parents. These young people should be welcomed into the church, where they find a plethora of fathers, mothers, brothers, and sisters in the faith (Ps. 82:3; Matt. 12:50; 1 Cor. 4:5; Phil. 2:22; 1 Thess. 2:11–12; 1 Tim. 1:2; 5:1–2; Titus 2:3–5; Philem. 1:10; James 1:27).

Fifth, I envision an emphasis on the gospel of grace in every area of church and family life, recognizing that we are all sinners in need of grace. Thus, this vision of church and home is not *law* driven, but *gospel* driven. God's commands simply point us to that which pleases the Lord. Your righteousness isn't found in being a good parent or spouse; it's found in Christ alone.

Most of us want to follow what God's design is for the church and home. We should strive to know His purpose and calling for us, even though we have long censored clear biblical instruction in this area. Again, we may not mean to, but many of us haven't really thought about it before. May we reclaim the joy and responsibility of bringing up our children in the instruction and discipline of the Lord.

TALKING POINTS

As parents, we have the privilege of investing our lives, our love, and our faith in the next generation. But this is not the way our culture views either parenting or children.

Children are a blessing from the Lord, and we have the loving responsibility to search the Scriptures on how to raise them for His glory.

The primary responsibility of our children's education does not fall on our president, the local baseball coach, or the youth pastor. The primary responsibility of our children's education falls on the parents.

DISCUSSION QUESTIONS

1. What are some evidences or examples in our culture that seem to devalue the blessing, privilege, and responsibility of raising children?

2. Can you think of a Bible verse that supports modern-day, age-segregated youth ministry?

3. What are some practical ways that the church and the home can complement each other in discipling children?

A FINAL WORD

Daring to Embrace the Entire Bible

This book has tried to expose our tendency to censor the offensive and difficult portions of Scripture and to demonstrate why such censorship leads to an unhealthy, unbalanced, and unfruitful faith. Rather than being embarrassed by these biblical texts, we have sought to embrace the entire Bible—"the whole counsel of God" (Acts 20:27)—for His glory and our joy in Him.

As we conclude, I want to give you a few takeaways on where to go from here; some practical steps on how to overcome our fear of man and our embarrassment of the Bible. I also want to briefly map out God's design for our continued growth in this area as followers of Jesus.

SECURE IN CHRIST

When I was a kid, I loved going to my grandparents' house. They had a log cabin nestled in the southern Appalachian Mountains at the end of a long gravel driveway. During the summer months, their garden sprang to life with huge cucumbers, squashes, tomatoes, and my favorite, raspberries. Granddad would spend his days splitting wood or tinkering with his tractor. Grandma stayed busy dehydrating food, grinding wheat, and mending worn-out clothes.

During the winter, their woodstove kept the house warm and toasty, and the family stayed close together. One thing that has stayed with me is their God-centeredness in just about everything they did. They woke up early every morning to read Scripture and pray together. They spoke of God as they sat in their house, as they walked by the way, and when they went to bed. It seemed as though their lives could have come straight out of Deuteronomy 6.

But more than all of this, I loved visiting them because their home radiated the warmth of love, godliness, and security. I didn't feel the need to pretend or perform to be somebody I wasn't. I didn't sense the anxiety of unhealthy competition over looks or abilities. I felt secure because of their constant love and care for me. Sure, I knew that they loved God and each other *more* than they loved me, but that rightly ordered love made me dwell in security and peace.

Oh, that we might sense the security and peace of knowing and having fellowship with our Lord Jesus. While my grandparents' house was (to me) a sanctuary of security in a hostile world, it has nothing on the security of being found in Christ. We've been given the greatest treasure that exists—God Himself—so that we might say, with the psalmist, "In your presence there is fullness of joy" (Ps. 16:11). There is joy because in Christ we have peace and reconciliation with God.

The apostle Paul knew what it felt like to be in want. He knew the pain of ridicule and loneliness. He also knew the physical pain of being stoned, beaten, and shipwrecked. While chained in prison, he recounted his many natural gifts and abilities (which we are prone to do) but exclaimed, "Whatever gain I had, I counted as loss for the sake of Christ. Indeed, I count everything as loss because of the surpassing worth of knowing Christ Jesus my Lord" (Phil. 3:7–8). What a profound and deep perspective to have on life!

The intimate relationship with Jesus is of *surpassing worth* to everything in this world—to vocations, vacations, bank accounts, status, and even family. What a place to anchor our hope and salvation! If God is for you, who can be against you? We can take rest in His promise: "For I am sure that neither death nor life, nor angels nor rulers, nor things present nor things to come, nor powers, nor height nor depth, nor anything else in all creation, will be able to separate us from the love of God in Christ Jesus our Lord" (Rom. 8:38–39).

When we behold the joy and security of knowing and having Christ, when we cultivate a right fear of and reverence for God, when we are humbled by His mercy in saving sinners like us, *the proclivity toward embarrassment of His Word falls down and blows away.* In that place of eternal security and the acknowledgment of the lordship of Jesus Christ over His universe, we move beyond the shadow of shame and dare to embrace the entire Bible because He is the everlasting King.

GROWING IN A FRUIT-BEARING FAITH

From that place of security and from the relational position of being God's adopted children, we are called to "grow in the grace and knowledge of our Lord" (2 Pet. 3:18). How do we grow and press on toward Christian maturity so as to produce spiritual and lasting fruit? What is God's design for our growth in grace?

Psalm 1 gives us a hint. There we find that a man is blessed when he doesn't follow the course of this world but rather takes his delight in the Word of God, meditating on it day and night. "He is like a tree planted by streams of water that yields its fruit in its season, and its leaf does not wither" (v. 3). Meditating on Scripture, memorizing it, and eagerly listening to it read and preached in worship plant the believer by streams of water.

In this way, God uses His Word to save and grow His people. The Scriptures are God's gift to us and to the body of Christ throughout the generations. Every jot and tittle of God's Word is "profitable for teaching, for reproof, for correction, and for training in righteousness" (2 Tim. 3:16). In the Scriptures, no word is missing and nothing is unimportant. While there are doctrines in the Bible that are of "first importance" (1 Cor. 15:3)—for example, Christ's death and resurrection—nothing is *un*important.

But if every word and doctrine has a holy significance in the Bible, and God uses His Word to grow us as His people, *then even the difficult and offensive portions are there for a reason*—that we might "all attain to the unity of the faith and of the knowledge of the Son of God, to mature manhood" (Eph. 4:13).

When we come to a Scripture passage that is offensive, we should pray and ask, "God, why have You inspired this text? What are You trying to teach Your church? How does this humble me and glorify Christ?" Let's take an example.

When we read that God commanded the Israelites to wipe out the Canaanites (Deut. 7), these are the questions we should ask.

We should come to see the severity of sin, the holiness and justice of God, and our need for a Savior. We should see that Israel, in and of itself, was no better than any other nation. In fact, in the very same chapter, we read, "It was not because you were more in number than any other people that the LORD set his love on you and chose you ... but it is because the LORD loves you" (vv. 7–8). We see here that God has all rights and all freedom. In no way does the punishment of sin and evil engender injustice on the part of God. On the contrary, it only confirms His righteous character.

But we shouldn't stop with the historic setting of Israel and the Canaanites. This text is given also for us as God's people throughout the ages. It should humble us and cause us to work out our salvation with fear and trembling (Phil. 2:12).

When we dare to embrace the entire Bible, God cultivates *in us* a fuller, more complete, and more God-honoring faith, "for it is God who works in you, both to will and to work for his good pleasure" (v. 13).

May we not be ashamed of the gospel or of God's Word. May we be "oaks of righteousness, the planting of the LORD, that he may be glorified" (Isa. 61:3). And may you rest in the security of knowing and being known by the eternal Christ, so that your hope is built on nothing less than His blood and righteousness.

ACKNOWLEDGMENTS

This book has not been easy to write, and I am grateful for the many people who endured lengthy discussions about its content and purpose. I'm thankful for my students at Reformed Theological Seminary in Atlanta, Georgia, who provided an atmosphere to work out some of these ideas in the context of historical theology. I'm thankful, too, for the elders and members at Wayside Presbyterian Church (PCA), where I pastor, for daring to embrace the entire Bible week by week in my sermons and affirming my ministry through writing. I'm also grateful for my agent, Chip MacGregor, who first latched on to the idea, and for Tim Peterson and the fine folks at David C Cook for patiently waiting to receive the manuscript. Most of all, I'd like to thank my bride, Ashley, for reading large portions of the book and constantly providing loving feedback.

NOTES

CHAPTER 2: AMERICA'S FIG-LEAF FAITH

1. "The Most and Least Bible-Minded Cities in the U.S. in 2014," American Bible Society, Barna Group, January 23, 2014, accessed May 5, 2015, http://cities.barna.org/americas-most-bible-minded-cities-2014/.

2. H. Richard Niebuhr, *The Kingdom of God in America* (Middletown, CT: Wesleyan University Press, 1988), 193.

3. Donald Grey Barnhouse, cited in Michael Horton, *Christless Christianity: The Alternative Gospel of the American Church* (Grand Rapids, MI: Baker Books, 2008), 15.

CHAPTER 3: BELIEVING GOD IN THE BIBLE

1. Mark Twain, quoted in Kelly M. Kapic and Randall C. Gleason, eds., *The Devoted Life: An Invitation to the Puritan Classics* (Downers Grove, IL: InterVarsity, 2004), 33.

2. Sometimes called "general revelation."

3. Louis Berkhof, *A Summary of Christian Doctrine* (Edinburgh: The Banner of Truth Trust, 2005), 12.

4. Geerhardus Vos, *Biblical Theology: Old and New Testaments* (Edinburgh: The Banner of Truth Trust, 1975), 13.

CHAPTER 4: WHY TRUST THE SCRIPTURES?

1. Some were combined (twelve Minor Prophets; histories of Samuel, Kings, Chronicles; Ezra–Nehemiah).

2. About 32 percent of the New Testament includes Old Testament material, quoting over 295 direct verses from the OT.

3. For support of some of this, see Michael J. Kruger, "A Christmas Present from the Mainstream Media: *Newsweek* Takes a Desperate Swipe at the Integrity of the Bible (Part 1)," Canon Fodder, December 24, 2014, http://michaeljkruger.com/a-christmas -present-from-the-mainstream-media-newsweek-takes-a-desperate-swipe-at-the -integrity-of-the-bible-part-1. He also referenced his book *Canon Revisited: Establishing the Origins and Authority of the New Testament Books* (Wheaton, IL: Crossway, 2012).

4. It should be noted that the Roman Catholic Church did not officially declare these to be Scripture until the Council of Trent (1545–63) as a *reaction* to the Protestant Reformation. This was meant to shore up certain Catholic doctrines (e.g., praying for the dead, purgatory, etc.). The word *Apocrypha* means "not canonical," from the Greek *apokryphos* ("obscure"). The Roman Church, however, calls these books "deuterocanonical books," or a "second canon."

5. The one exception is in the book of Jude, which quotes from Enoch (see v. 14). Paul quoted pagan authors (Acts 17:28), but neither assumes divine authority or canonicity.

6. See Josh McDowell, *Evidence That Demands a Verdict* (Nashville: Thomas Nelson, 1979), 39–78.

7. See John H. Armstrong, "The Authority of Scripture" in *Sola Scriptura!* (Morgan, PA: Soli Deo Gloria, 1995), 104. He also noted that the New Testament has several repeated phrases, such as "Scripture says" and "According to the scriptures."

8. Some of these references include: Genesis 2:24 (Matt. 19:4–5); Psalms 2:1–2, 7 (Acts 4:24–25; Heb. 1:5); 16:10 (Acts 13:35); 95:7–11 (Heb. 3:7–11); 97:7 (Heb. 1:6); 104:4 (Heb. 1:7); and Isaiah 55:3 (Acts 13:34). For the interchangeability of "scrip- ture" and "God," see John W. Wenham, "Christ's View of Scripture," in Norman L. Geisler, ed., *Inerrancy* (Grand Rapids, MI: Zondervan, 1980), 21–22.

9. For a good review of this, see John Piper, *Why We Believe the Bible* (Wheaton, IL: Crossway, 2009), 91–93.

10. See Sam Harris, *The Moral Landscape: How Science Can Determine Human Values* (New York: Free Press, 2010).

11. A quote from the famous atheist Bertrand Russell (1872–1970) in his *Mysticism and Logic* (New York: W. W. Norton, 1929), 48.

CHAPTER 5: STONING THE ADULTERER: THE UNITY OF SCRIPTURE

1. Tim Keller, "Making Sense of Scripture's 'Inconsistency,'" The Gospel Coalition, July 9, 2012, accessed May 6, 2015, www.thegospelcoalition.org/article/making -sense-of-scriptures-inconsistency.

2. The best study Bible available, in my opinion, is the ESV Study Bible. It's very large, no doubt, but it's full of helpful articles, charts, introductions, and commentary.

3. Jonathan Edwards (1703–1758), the First Great Awakening revivalist preacher of New England, wrote a treatise on this entitled The End for Which God Created the World. The complete text may be found in John Piper, God's Passion for His Glory: Living the Vision of Jonathan Edwards (Wheaton, IL: Crossway, 2006).

4. To be exact, there is also the covenant of redemption between the persons of the Godhead for the salvation of the elect. For the purposes of this chapter, however, I'll be focusing on just the various covenants between God and His people.

5. Adam's relationship with God is actually called a "covenant" in Hosea 6:7. This covenant is oftentimes called the covenant of life or the covenant of works.

6. The word testament is another word for covenant.

CHAPTER 6: MAKING GOD IN OUR IMAGE

1. John Piper and Justin Taylor, eds., A God-Entranced Vision of All Things: The Legacy of Jonathan Edwards (Wheaton, IL: Crossway, 2004).

2. Jonathan Edwards, "A Dissertation on the End for Which God Created the World," in The Works of Jonathan Edwards, vol. 1 (Edinburgh: Banner of Truth Trust, 1974), 120.

3. Westminster Shorter Catechism, Q1.

4. Bob Smietana, "Americans Believe in Heaven, Hell, and a Little Bit of Heresy," LifeWay Research, October 28, 2014, accessed May 7, 2015, www.lifewayresearch.com/2014 /10/28/americans-believe-in-heaven-hell-and-a-little-bit-of-heresy/.

5. As seen in the problematic book by Harold S. Kushner, When Bad Things Happen to Good People (New York: Schocken Books, 1981).

6. For a more in-depth study, see Brian H. Cosby, Be Still and Know: Meditations on the Character of God (Bloomington, IN: Westbow, 2011); and Arthur W. Pink, The Attributes of God (Grand Rapids, MI: Baker Books, 2006).

7. The Greek word for *saints* in the New Testament literally means "holy ones" (cf. Phil. 1:1; Col. 1:2). Moreover, Christians are set apart as a "holy nation" (1 Pet. 2:9).

8. John Piper, *God's Passion for His Glory: Living the Vision of Jonathan Edwards* (Wheaton, IL: Crossway, 2006), 34–35.

9. R. C. Sproul, *The Character of God: Discovering the God Who Is* (Ventura, CA: Regal, 1995), 84.

CHAPTER 7: COVERING UP CREATION

1. Peter Enns, *The Bible Tells Me So: Why Defending Scripture Has Made Us Unable to Read It* (New York: HarperOne, 2014).

2. Enns, *Bible Tells Me So*, front flap. The reference is to Rob Bell, *Love Wins: A Book about Heaven, Hell, and the Fate of Every Person Who Ever Lived* (New York: HarperOne, 2011).

3. Enns, *Bible Tells Me So*, 4.

4. Enns, *Bible Tells Me So*, 5–6.

5. One of the best resources, though it is rather technical, is Terry Mortenson and Thane H. Ury, eds., *Coming to Grips with Genesis: Biblical Authority and the Age of the Earth* (Green Forest, AR: Master Books, 2008).

6. For a scholarly breakdown of this statistical data and its analysis, see Steven W. Boyd, "Statistical Determination of Genre in Biblical Hebrew: Evidence for an Historical Reading of Genesis 1:1–2:3," in *Radioisotopes and the Age of the Earth: Results of a Young-Earth Creationist Research Initiative*, vol. 2, ed. Larry Vardiman, et al. (San Diego: Institute for Creation Research, 2005).

7. There are over one hundred quotes or direct references to Genesis in the NT, none of them supposing myth or allegory. For some examples that reference the creation account and early chapters of Genesis, see Matthew 19:5; 24:37–38; Mark 10:6–7; 13:19; Luke 11:50–51; 13:14; John 5:45–47; Colossians 1:16–17; and 2 Peter 3:5–6.

8. Walter C. Kaiser, *Old Testament Documents: Are They Reliable and Relevant?* (Downers Grove, IL: InterVarsity, 2001), 82.

9. Some cite 2 Peter 3:8, saying that God's days are like a thousand years; therefore, the "days" in Genesis are long ages. This is a reference to the judgment of Christ's second coming.

10. Some might (falsely) contend that people and animals ate plants before the fall and, as a result, there was "death" of plants. But the Hebrew word designating "life" (*nephesh*) was never used of plants, only of people and animals. Plants are not "alive" in the way people or animals are "alive." Plants were given for food. Man was permitted to eat meat only after the flood (cf. Gen. 9:3).

11. Stephen C. Meyer, *Darwin's Doubt: The Explosive Origin of Animal Life and the Case for Intelligent Design* (New York: HarperOne, 2013).

12. Ken Ham is well known for making this statement or versions of it. Even early Christians attributed the fossils they observed with the Noahic flood, including Tertullian, Chrysostom, and Augustine.

13. Dr. Jason Lisle (PhD in astrophysics from the University of Colorado) has helped immensely in this area of astronomy and the "problem" of distant starlight. You can find out more about his work at icr.org.

14. George William Hunter, *A Civic Biology: Presented in Problems* (New York: American Book Company, 1914), 196, emphasis mine.

CHAPTER 8: MASKING THE REALITY OF SIN

1. Bob Smietana, "Americans Believe in Heaven, Hell, and a Little Bit of Heresy," LifeWay Research, October 28, 2014, accessed May 9, 2015, www.lifewayresearch.com/2014/10/28/americans-believe-in-heaven-hell-and-a-little-bit-of-heresy/.

2. Actual quote: "Your thoughts concerning God are too human." Martin Luther, *The Bondage of the Will* (Lafayette, IN: Sovereign Grace, 2001), 22.

3. David Platt, *Follow Me: A Call to Die. A Call to Live.* (Carol Stream, IL: Tyndale, 2013), 31.

CHAPTER 9: TURNING A BLIND EYE TO SUFFERING

1. For a broader study of the material in this chapter, see Brian H. Cosby, *A Christian's Pocket Guide to Suffering* (Ross-shire, UK: Christian Focus, 2015).

2. Richard Dawkins, *River Out of Eden: A Darwinian View of Life* (New York: Basic Books, 1995), 131, 133.

3. Bertrand Russell, *Mysticism and Logic and Other Essays* (New York: Longmans, Green, 1919), 48.

4. *Omnipresence* means that the creator God is present everywhere (Job 34:21; Ps. 139:7–10; Prov. 15:3; Jer. 23:24; Matt. 18:20).

5. Some of the material in this section is taken from Brian H. Cosby, "Why Does God Ordain Suffering? A Puritan's Answer," in *Evangelical Times*, August 2013.

6. For more about John Flavel, see Brian H. Cosby, *John Flavel: Puritan Life and Thought in Stuart England* (Lanham, MD: Lexington Books, 2014).

7. For a more detailed analysis of this, see Brian H. Cosby, *Suffering and Sovereignty: John Flavel and the Puritans on Afflictive Providence* (Grand Rapids, MI: Reformation Heritage Books, 2012).

8. John Flavel, *A Token for Mourners*, in *The Works of John Flavel*, 6 vols. (Edinburgh: Banner of Truth, 1968), 5:605–6.

9. Flavel, *Divine Conduct*, 4:407.

10. Flavel, *Preparation for Sufferings*, 6:9–10.

11. Flavel, *Divine Conduct*, 4:429–30.

12. Flavel, *Divine Conduct*, 4:442.

13. Flavel, *Navigation Spiritualized*, 5:252.

14. Flavel, *Preparation for Sufferings*, 6:11.

15. From his hymn "A Mighty Fortress Is Our God."

CHAPTER 10: HIDING THE HORRORS OF HELL

1. Bob Smietana, "Americans Believe in Heaven, Hell, and a Little Bit of Heresy," LifeWay Research, October 28, 2014, accessed May 10, 2015, www.lifewayresearch.com/2014/10/28/americans-believe-in-heaven-hell-and-a-little-bit-of-heresy/.

2. John Gerstner, quoted in R. C. Sproul, *Unseen Realities: Heaven, Hell, Angels, and Demons* (Ross-shire, UK: Christian Focus, 2011), 53.

3. Jonathan Merritt, "Tony Campolo's Surprise Reaction When His Son Came Out as a Humanist," Aquila Report, October 12, 2014, accessed May 10, 2015, http://theaquilareport.com/tony-campolos-surprise-reaction-when-his-son-came-out-as-a-humanist/.

4. Both books were published by David C Cook in 2011.

5. Francis Chan and Preston Sprinkle, *Erasing Hell: What God Said about Eternity, and the Things We've Made Up* (Colorado Springs: David C Cook, 2011), 108.

6. Timothy Keller, *The Reason for God: Belief in an Age of Skepticism* (New York: Dutton, 2008), 9.

7. John Calvin, *The Institutes of the Christian Religion*, vol. 2, ed. John T. McNeill, trans. Ford Lewis Battles (Philadelphia: Westminster John Knox, 1960), 16:8–10.

8. For a good resource on this debate, see Daniel R. Hyde, *In Defense of the Descent: A Response to Contemporary Critics* (Grand Rapids, MI: Reformation Heritage Books, 2010).

9. Brian Jones, *Hell Is Real (But I Hate to Admit It)* (Colorado Springs: David C Cook, 2011), 102.

CHAPTER 11: GOING AFTER GIMMICKS: "SUCCESS" IN THE ENTERTAINMENT CHURCH

1. For a similar description, see Brian H. Cosby, "Church Gimmicks and the Idol of Success," *Credo Magazine*, April 2014.

2. John Piper, *When the Darkness Will Not Lift: Doing What We Can While We Wait for God—and Joy* (Wheaton, IL: Crossway, 2006), 61–62.

3. Similarly related, M. Scott Peck defined the will as "desire of sufficient intensity that it is translated into action" (*The Road Less Traveled: A New Psychology of Love, Traditional Values, and Spiritual Growth* [New York: Touchstone, 2003], 83).

CHAPTER 12: DON'T TRY THIS AT HOME: OUTSOURCING PARENTING

1. Harvey S. Wiener, *Talk with Your Child* (New York: Viking, 1988), n.p.

2. Scripture passages on the varying roles: Genesis 2:18–24; 1 Corinthians 11:3–12; Ephesians 5:22–33; Colossians 3:18–21; 1 Timothy 2:11–13; Titus 2:1–5; 1 Peter 3:1–7.

3. John Piper, *What's the Difference?: Manhood and Womanhood Defined according to the Bible* (Wheaton, IL: Crossway, 1990), 22.

4. John Piper, "Husbands Who Love Like Christ and the Wives Who Submit to Them," Desiring God, June 11, 1989, accessed May 11, 2015, www.desiringgod.org/sermons /husbands-who-love-like-christ-and-the-wives-who-submit-to-them.

5. Cheryl Wetzstein, "US Fertility Plummets to Record Low," *Washington Times*, May 28, 2014, www.washingtontimes.com/news/2014/may/28 /us-birthrate-plummets-to-record-low/?page=all.

6. Douglas Wilson, *Father Hunger: Why God Calls Men to Love and Lead Their Families* (Nashville: Thomas Nelson, 2012).

7. US Census Bureau, "American Families and Living Arrangements: 2013," accessed at census.gov.

8. From Population Reference Bureau, analysis of data from the US Census Bureau, Census 2000 Supplementary Survey, 2001 Supplementary Survey, 2002 through 2012 American Community Survey, accessed at datacenter.kidscount.org.

9. Kirsten Andersen, "The Number of US Children Living in Single-Parent Homes Has Nearly Doubled in 50 Years: Census Data," January 4, 2013, accessed May 11, 2015, www.lifesitenews.com/news/the-number-of-children-living-in-single-parent-home -has-nearly-doubled-in.

10. Voddie Baucham, "Thoughts on Ferguson," The Gospel Coalition, November 26, 2014, www.thegospelcoalition.org/article/thoughts-on-ferguson.

11. Melissa Harris-Perry, MSNBC video release, April 4, 2013.